S0-ASF-869

Women of Destiny

Women of Destiny

REFLECTIONS ON THE
RELIEF SOCIETY DECLARATION

COMPILED BY JENNIE J. FORD

EAGLE GATE

SALT LAKE CITY, UTAH

© 2002 Deseret Book Company

All rights reserved. No part of this book may be reproduced in any form or by any means without permission in writing from the publisher, Deseret Book Company, P. O. Box 30178, Salt Lake City, Utah 84130. This work is not an official publication of The Church of Jesus Christ of Latter-day Saints. The views expressed herein are the responsibility of the authors and do not necessarily represent the position of the Church or of Deseret Book Company.

Eagle Gate is a registered trademark of Deseret Book Company.

Visit us at www.deseretbook.com

Library of Congress Cataloging-in-Publication Data

Women of destiny : reflections on the Relief Society declaration /
    Compiled by Jennie Ford.
        p.   cm.
    Includes index.
    ISBN 1-57008-864-0 (hardbound : alk. paper)
    1. Mormon women—Religious life.   2. Relief Society (Church of Jesus
Christ of Latter-day Saints)   I. Ford, Jennie.
    BX8643.W4 W67   2002
    267'.449332—dc21   2002013814

Printed in the United States of America   72076-7000
Publishers Printing, Salt Lake City, Utah

10 9   8   7   6   5   4   3   2   1

CONTENTS

Contents

CONTENTS

Contents

Contents

CONTENTS

CONTENTS

INTRODUCTION

As women in The Church of Jesus Christ of Latter-day Saints, we are sisters in Relief Society, which was divinely organized to help us recognize and use our unique gifts as daughters of our Heavenly Father. "Each of us has a vital role, even a sacred mission to perform as a daughter in Zion. It is a new day, the dawning of a new era. It is our time, and it is our destiny to rejoice as we fill the earth with greater kindness and gentleness, greater love and compassion, greater sympathy and empathy than has ever been known before. It is time to give ourselves to the Master and allow Him to lead us into fruitful fields where we can enrich a world filled with darkness and misery" (Mary Ellen Smoot, "Rejoice, Daughters of Zion," *Ensign,* November 1999, 94).

Sisters in Relief Society today are truly women of destiny, women who can exert great power and influence on the earth. We have come forth at this time to combat the evil influence of Satan with the spirit of good, to raise a standard of righteousness in the world. We have been sent by our Father to reach out with charity and bless the lives of those we serve. We emulate the love of the Savior by humbly following his example and seeking his comfort and direction. Individual in our talents, appearance, and life circumstances, we are united by the strength of a sisterhood bound in friendship and eternal love.

The Relief Society Declaration, presented in a general Relief Society meeting on 25 September 1999, has a two-fold purpose: "to respond to queries from outside the Church, and to remind ourselves of the grand blessing of womanhood." Each principle of the declaration will help us "like Father Lehi, have a hope that as we journey along our path of life, we will partake of the fruit found in this gospel of Jesus Christ in personal ways and experience joy that will fill our souls with greater faith, hope, and charity" (Smoot, "Rejoice, Daughters of Zion," 92–93).

The selections in this volume will help us catch a vision of our eternal worth as women of destiny. We will gain a better understanding of the uplifting principles found in the Declaration and how we might always have his Spirit to be with us. Our Father wants us to be happy, and he longs to embrace us in the arms of his love.

Our sisterhood in Relief Society will help sustain us in difficult times, help teach us who we are, and help us develop our talents through faith, learning, and service. By studying and living the principles of the Declaration, we will grow closer to our Savior and our Heavenly Father, who will strengthen our powerful and joyful influence for good.

Part One

We Are Daughters of God
United in Our Devotion
to Jesus Christ

OUR TRUE SELVES

Patricia T. Holland

Surely there has not been another time in history when women have questioned their self-worth as harshly and critically as they do today. Many women are searching, almost frantically, as never before, for a sense of personal purpose and meaning; and many Latter-day Saint women are searching, too, for eternal insight and meaning in their femaleness.

If I were Satan and wanted to destroy a society, I think I would stage a full-blown blitz on women. I would keep them so distraught and distracted that they would never find the calming strength and serenity for which their sex has always been known.

Satan has effectively done that, catching us in the crunch of trying to be superhuman instead of striving to reach our unique, God-given potential within such diversity. He tauntingly teases us

---

Patricia Terry Holland has served as first counselor in the Young Women general presidency. She and her husband, Elder Jeffrey R. Holland of the Quorum of the Twelve Apostles, are the parents of three children.

that if we don't have it all—fame, fortune, families, and fun, and have it all the time—we have been short-changed and are second-class citizens in the race of life. As a sex we are struggling, our families are struggling, and our society is struggling. Drugs, teenage pregnancies, divorce, family violence, and suicide are some of the ever-increasing side effects of our collective life in the express lane.

Too many of us are struggling and suffering, too many are running faster than they have strength, expecting *too* much of themselves. As a result, we are experiencing many stress-related illnesses. One such disease was described more than two decades ago: "[Its victims] are plagued by low-grade fevers, aching joints, and sometimes a sore throat—but they don't have the flu. They're overwhelmingly exhausted, weak, and debilitated—but they don't have AIDS. They're often confused and forgetful—but it isn't Alzheimer's. Many patients feel suicidal, but it isn't clinical depression. . . . Female victims outnumber males about 3 to 1, and a great many are intelligent high achievers with stressful lives" (*Newsweek*, 27 October 1986, 105).

We *must* have the courage to be imperfect while striving for perfection. We *must* not allow our own guilt, the feminist books, the talk-show hosts, or the whole media culture to sell us a bill of goods—or rather, a bill of *no* goods. We can become so sidetracked in our compulsive search for identity and self-esteem that we really believe it *can* be found in having perfect figures or academic degrees or professional status or even absolute motherly success. Yet, in so searching externally, we can be torn from our true internal, eternal selves. We often worry so much about pleasing and performing for others that we lose our uniqueness—that full and relaxed acceptance of one's self as a person of worth and individuality. We become so frightened and insecure that we cannot be generous toward the diversity and individuality, and yes, problems, of our neighbors. Too many women with these anxieties watch helplessly as their lives unravel from the very core that centers and sustains them. Too many are like a ship at sea without sail or rudder, "tossed to and fro," as the apostle Paul said (Ephesians 4:14), until more and more of us are genuinely, rail-grabbingly seasick.

Where is the sureness that allows us to sail our ship, whatever winds may blow, with the master seaman's triumphant cry, "Steady as she goes"? Where is the inner stillness we so cherish and for which our sex traditionally has been known?

I believe we can find our steady footing and stilling of the soul by turning away from physical preoccupations, superwoman accomplishments, and endless popularity contests, and returning instead to the wholeness of our soul, that unity in our very being that balances the demanding and inevitable diversity of life.

I know that God loves us individually and collectively *as women* and that he has a mission for every one of us. I testify that if our desires are righteous, God overrules for our good and that heavenly parents will tenderly attend to our needs. In our diversity and individuality, my prayer is that we will be united—united in seeking *our* specific, foreordained mission, united in asking *not*, "What can the kingdom do for me?" but "What can I do for the kingdom? How can I fulfill the measure of *my* creation? In my circumstances and with my challenges and my faith, where is my *full* realization of the godly image in which I was created?"

With faith in God, his prophets, his Church, and ourselves—with faith in our own divine creation—may we be peaceful and let go of our cares and troubles over so many things. May we believe—nothing doubting—in the light that shines, even in a dark place.

———

See Patricia T. Holland, "'One Thing Needful': Becoming Women of Greater Faith in Christ," Ensign, October 1987, 26.

LIVE EACH DAY WITHOUT REGRET

Mary Ellen Smoot

Occasionally I place my hands on both sides of the face of one of my children or grandchildren when they are doing something that will bring immediate or long-term harm to themselves in the process. I look deeply into their eyes and carefully explain to them how much they are loved and cherished. Then I describe the harm that could result from the actions they have chosen.

I can envision the Savior holding our faces between his hands and pleading with each of us individually to remain steadfast and immovable and faithful to the God who made us.

Before coming into this mortal world, we lived together in the presence of a loving Heavenly Father. I imagine one of our

---

Mary Ellen Smoot, who loves family history and has written several histories of parents, grandparents, and their local community, has served as general president of the Relief Society. She served with her husband, Stanley M. Smoot, when he was called as mission president in Ohio. They are the parents of seven children.

favorite topics of conversation was what would happen when we passed through the veil and entered this earthly existence.

Now we are here. Even though we were instructed regarding the difficulties we would encounter on earth, I doubt we understood or could have known how demanding and trying, how tiring and even sorrowful at times this mortal existence would be. We have no doubt all, at some point, felt that what we were experiencing was just too hard to bear.

I can imagine our Savior placing his hands on both sides of our faces, looking deeply into our eyes, and promising a sisterhood, a Relief Society, to help us in our trials. This organization for all women of the Church is for the purpose of helping to bring us to the Savior and assisting one another in helping the sick and the poor.

President Gordon B. Hinckley has counseled the women of the Church: "Rise to the great potential within you. I do not ask that you reach beyond your capacity. I hope you will not nag yourselves with thoughts of failure. I hope you will not try to set goals far beyond your capacity to achieve. I hope you will simply do what you can do in the best way you know. If you do so, you will witness miracles come to pass" (*Motherhood, a Heritage of Faith* [Salt Lake City: Deseret Book, 1995], 9).

When I hear sisters say, "It is just too hard to do my visiting teaching" or "I simply do not have time to pray and read my scriptures!" or "I have too much going on to attend home, family, and personal enrichment meeting," I want to say as President Hinckley has counseled, "Rise to the great potential within you." We may need to step back and consider if our actions are consistent with those things that matter most to us. As we place first things first in our lives, we can live each day without regret.

———

See Mary Ellen Smoot, "Steadfast and Immovable," Ensign, November 2001, 91.

Noble and Great

Carol B. Thomas

It was my father who taught me about the premortal life. He explained that long ago you and I were born as daughters in our Heavenly Father's family. We made sacred decisions there that have influenced what we are doing now. When I was younger, my grandfather gave me a blessing. He blessed me to "continue my ministry here that I had so nobly performed there." Now, if I had a ministry in the premortal existence, then so did you. It is not by chance that we were born now, in this season of the world's history. Each one of us was a valiant and noble woman in our premortal life.

Abraham said, "Now the Lord had shown unto me, Abraham, the intelligences that were organized before the world was; and

---

Carol Burdett Thomas has served as a member of the general board of the Relief Society and as first counselor in the Young Women general presidency. She and her husband, D. Ray Thomas, are the parents of seven children.

among all these . . . were many of the noble and great ones" (Abraham 3:22). Do you know that he was talking about you? We are each noble and great, born to live at this time on the earth.

We all come from many different kinds of families. Some are doing hard things and doing them so very well. Some may worry about relationships as we learn together how to live in families. We are learning that sometimes the Savior calms the storm. Sometimes he lets the storm rage, and he calms us.

Paraphrasing what Elder Jeffrey R. Holland once said, "The [home] is not a monastery for perfect people"; sometimes it is a hospital where we nurse and take care of those we love ("'He Hath Filled the Hungry with Good Things,'" *Ensign,* November 1997, 66).

One young woman wrote: "Every person in my family has hard times, but I try to be there for them and help them out. . . . We want to be together for all eternity."

Feelings were nurtured in our souls long before we came to this earth. President Gordon B. Hinckley has said, "Women, for the most part, see their greatest fulfillment, their greatest happiness in home and family" (*Teachings of Gordon B. Hinckley* [Salt Lake City: Deseret Book, 1997], 387).

As we pray and read our scriptures and keep the commandments, the Holy Ghost will whisper to us that we belong to Heavenly Father's royal family and that he loves us very much.

———

See Carol B. Thomas, "Understanding Our True Identity," Ensign, May 1998, 91.

THE FATHER'S LOVE

Jayne B. Malan

There's something magic about sleeping under the stars at a Young Women camp, especially on a dark night when there's no moon and the stars are bright. It's a perfect setting for quiet talks about things that matter most and for music. No matter how tired the girls may be, there's music—little groups singing somewhere in the dark as they settle in for the night—and, at times, the far-away sound of a ukulele or guitar. I found that sleeping outside keeps one closer to the action when someone needs help or comfort or counsel in the middle of the night.

It had been a night such as this that last year I went to camp. About the time the last tearful campers were tucked into bed and the camp was finally quiet, I noticed the first hint of morning in the sky. We had been looking for a place to hold a sunrise service,

Jayne B. Malan has served on the general boards of the Relief Society and the Young Women and as second counselor in the Young Women general presidency. She and her husband, Terry Malan, are the parents of two children.

and because I was still awake, this seemed to be the perfect time to find it. So I slipped out of my sleeping bag and headed up a little trail through the trees. Coming up over a small rise, I found a grassy meadow where you could look out over the valley and the mountains to the north. I stood there for a long time watching the sky grow lighter and the clouds turn from gray to pink and then white.

As it grew light, the mountains across the valley seemed in some way to be familiar to me even though I had never been in this location before. I dismissed the thought at first and then realized that I was looking at the back side of the same mountains that I knew so very well from a different viewpoint. These were the mountains that I could see from my bedroom window at the ranch when I was a child growing up. Many times I had watched them change color on stormy days as clouds would gather over them, and the rain came down the valley where our ranch was located.

Memories flooded back of my mother and father and their love for me. I thought of my Heavenly Father and how he had blessed me. As I stood there watching the sunrise, I could feel the warmth of the Savior's loving, guiding hand. I knew without being told that I was a literal daughter of God and, because of the sacrifice of his Son, I can be with my earthly parents again some day and live in the presence of our Heavenly Father. I had taught this truth many times to others, but this morning it seemed as if I had discovered it for the first time. Perhaps I really had. I had received a witness of the Spirit.

Standing on that hilltop, I thanked my Heavenly Father for what I knew. And I promised to dedicate my life to his service. I can't express the joy of that moment. I wanted to hurry back to camp and wake everyone up. I wanted to tell them who they really are, daughters of God! I wanted to tell them to have faith, to talk to our Heavenly Father—to stop worrying about little things or things they can't change. I wanted them to know that God lives and watches over us, and through his Son, Jesus Christ, all things are possible. All he asks is that we do the best we can with what we have and stay close to him. I wanted to tell them, "You're a daughter of God, and he loves you. He needs you—every one of you! Do you know that?"

———

See Jayne B. Malan, "These Are Your Days," Ensign, November 1991, 92.

ALL WE HAVE TO GIVE HIM

Sheri Dew

I have come to believe that whatever we really want, we'll probably get. If we really want money and status, we'll find a way to get them. By the same token, if we really want to overcome bad habits or cultivate integrity or become more pure so that we can better hear the voice of the Spirit, we'll find a way to do those things as well. Fifty years from now what we have become shouldn't surprise us, because we will have become what we have set our hearts upon.

Alma taught that the Lord "granteth unto men according to their desire" (Alma 29:4). And when asked to identify the first great commandment, the Savior said simply, "Thou shalt love the Lord thy God with all thy heart, and with all thy soul, and with

Sheri Dew has served as second counselor in the Relief Society general presidency. A graduate of Brigham Young University in history and a best-selling author, she serves as president of Deseret Book Company.

all thy mind" (Matthew 22:37). It's no accident that our hearts were mentioned first.

Satan is also after our hearts, because he knows that if he can control our feelings and desires, he can control us—which is why he tries to harden our hearts, puff up the pride of our hearts, and set our hearts upon the vain things of the world (4 Nephi 1:28; 2 Nephi 33:2; 28:15; Helaman 12:4). The Nephite civilization collapsed entirely once the people were past feeling (Moroni 9:20). Likewise, we have been warned that in the last days "men's hearts will fail them" (D&C 88:91), and the nightly news verifies this sad reality. Children killing children. "Spin doctors" celebrated for their articulate cunning rather than censored for breaches of integrity. Violence that knows no bounds.

No wonder we are commanded to "come unto the Lord with all [our hearts]" (Mormon 9:27). No wonder the Lord "requireth the heart and a willing mind" (D&C 64:34). Notice that He said nothing about how gorgeous or thin or educated or affluent we must be. He simply asks for our hearts and our will, because that's all we have to give Him. Everything else is already His. Said Brigham Young, "The Lord must be first and foremost in our affections; the building up of his cause and kingdom demands our first consideration" (*Deseret News Weekly,* 5 January 1854, 2). Ultimately we will become what we give our hearts to, for we are shaped by what we desire and seek after. If we love the Lord such that our hearts are changed, His image will fill our countenances. But if we love the world more, we'll slowly take upon us those characteristics. As Truman Madsen has remarked, "At youth our face reveals genetics. At fifty, we have the face we deserve."

The question we might therefore want to ponder is simply this: What do we really want? And what are we willing to do to get it? When we were baptized, we said we wanted to come into the fold of God (Mosiah 18:8). But do we really? Do we delight in being called His people, though that probably means looking and acting and dressing differently from the rest of the world? If so, are we willing to yield our hearts to the Lord? Those who do will be born again as the sons and daughters of Christ (Mosiah 5:7). The choice is ours. What we really want, we'll ultimately get.

––––––

See Sheri Dew, "Shall We Not Go Forward in So Great a Cause?" Arise and Shine Forth (Salt Lake City: Deseret Book, 2001), 21.

Part Two

We Are Women of Faith,
Virtue, Vision, and
Charity

FAITH WILL CONQUER FEAR

Virginia H. Pearce

As we read the scriptures, we find that fear has been a part of the history of individuals ever since the world began. I can even imagine that in the preexistent world, when the two plans were presented, some may have chosen Lucifer's plan because of fear—the fear of leaving the presence of the Father with no guarantee that we would return. Lucifer perhaps played on those fears by assuring that with his plan, all would return.

I can imagine how frightening it must have been for Adam and Eve, who had lived with complete security—friendly animals, plenty to eat, no opposition from nature—to suddenly be cast into a world where survival itself must have been a constant fear.

Why is fear part of earth life?

Virginia H. Pearce, who received a master's degree in social work from the University of Utah, has served as first counselor in the Young Women general presidency. She and her husband, James R. Pearce, are the parents of six children.

Perhaps our Heavenly Father's greatest hope is that through our fears we may choose to turn to him. The uncertainties of earth life can help to remind each of us that we are dependent on him. But that reminder is not automatic. It involves our agency. We must *choose* to take our fears to him, *choose* to trust him, and *choose* to allow him to direct us. We must make these choices when what we feel most inclined to do is to rely more and more on our own frantic and often distorted thinking.

As we try to live his commandments and pray to him, there are things he will direct us to do that will help calm our fears. These actions often require great courage and direction from the Holy Ghost. The Holy Ghost may help us to understand when and with whom we should share our fears. He will support us as we face our fears and try to do things that we have never done before.

As women, we like very much to please others—sometimes seeking approval so frantically that we become torn and confused by the conflicting needs of those around us. Concentrating on pleasing Heavenly Father brings peace, a respite from fear and anxiety. The prophet David said: "The Lord is my light and my salvation; whom shall I fear? the Lord is the strength of my life; of whom shall I be afraid?" (Psalm 27:1).

It is reported that Vincent van Gogh, the famous painter, said, "I am always doing what I can't do yet in order to learn how to do it." A large part of conquering daily fear is simply doing things that we don't know how to do—yet.

Eleanor Roosevelt was the wife of a president of the United States, but her influence went far beyond politics and position. Her life is a beacon to all women as someone who magnificently developed her own gifts through service to others. This woman's early life was ruled by fear and self-doubt. She described herself as an awkward adolescent, unattractively tall, with protruding teeth, dressed inappropriately, and so ill at ease with others her own age that parties and dances were dreaded occasions. How did she move from that to the kind of confidence that allowed her to contribute so widely?

She said, "You gain strength, courage, and confidence by every experience in which you really stop to look fear in the face. You must do the thing which you think you cannot do" (Karen McAuley, *Eleanor Roosevelt* [New York: Chelsea House, 1987], 105).

As we concentrate on pleasing the Lord rather than others and continue to work hard, doing the things we don't know how to do yet, we will experience personal growth. We will increase our confidence in Heavenly Father and his Son, Jesus Christ. This faith assures us that in the end, we will not only survive but we will know great joy and happiness.

See Virginia H. Pearce, "Fear," Ensign, November 1992, 90.

TRUST IN THE LORD

Barbara B. Ballard

Some people carry a real burden through life; but I believe that if we look deep enough, all of us face our own set of challenges that we must handle in our own way. This life truly is a proving ground for each of us.

Brigham Young wrote: "You all know that the Saints must be made pure, to enter into the celestial kingdom. It is recorded that Jesus was made perfect through suffering. If he was made perfect through suffering, why should we imagine for one moment that we can be prepared to enter into the kingdom of rest with him and the Father, without passing through similar ordeals?" (*Discourses of Brigham Young,* sel. John A. Widtsoe [Salt Lake City: Deseret Book, 1954], 346).

Barbara Bowen Ballard has served as a teacher or officer in every Church auxiliary. She served with her husband, Elder M. Russell Ballard, later a member of the Quorum of the Twelve Apostles, while he presided over the Canada Toronto Mission. They are the parents of seven children.

A great example of a woman who gained such pure faith is Mary Fielding Smith, wife of Hyrum Smith, older brother of the Prophet Joseph. She is my husband's great-great-grandmother and a remarkable example of courage, inner strength, and faith.

When Joseph and Hyrum were martyred in Carthage Jail, Hyrum's wife, Mary, was left on her own with a large family to care for. Notwithstanding her many challenges, she decided to travel west with the Saints. In her history, she records her extremely trying and difficult circumstances that would have discouraged most women as she journeyed in a wagon train headed for the Salt Lake Valley from Winter Quarters. Even the captain of the wagon train, who resented her being there, tried to weaken her resolve to go on.

You may be familiar with her experience "at a point midway between the Platte and the Sweetwater rivers, when one of Mary's best oxen lay down in the yoke as if poisoned and all supposed he would die. All the teams [behind her] stopped, and many gathered around to see what had happened. In a short time, the Captain perceived that something was wrong and came to the spot. The ox stiffened in the throes of death. The Captain blustered about and exclaimed: 'He is dead; there is no use working with him, we'll have to fix up some way to take the Widow along. I told her she would be a burden on the company.' But in this, he was greatly mistaken.

"Mary said nothing but went to her wagon and returned with a bottle of consecrated oil. She asked her brother Joseph and [his friend] James Lawson to administer to her fallen ox, believing that the Lord would raise him. It was a solemn moment there under the open sky. A hush fell over the scene. The men removed their hats. All bowed their heads as Joseph Fielding . . . knelt, laid his hands on the head of the prostrate ox, and prayed over it. The great beast lay stretched out and very still. Its glassy eyes looked nowhere. A moment after the administration the animal stirred. . . . Its haunches started to rise. The forelegs strengthened. The ox stood and, without urging, started off as if nothing had happened. This amazing thing greatly astonished the onlookers" (Don Cecil Corbett, *Mary Fielding Smith, Daughter of Britain* [Salt Lake City: Deseret Book, 1966], 236–37). The team went on with a renewal of strength for the remainder of the long journey.

Mary's great faith touched her young son Joseph's heart, and he never forgot his mother's example. Her great faith helped carry Joseph F. through a lifetime of dedicated service, including serving as president of the Church for seventeen years. I believe that all mothers can leave a legacy of faith for their children if they themselves have that faith.

Their indomitable courage came from their unwavering faith. As with them, so it is with us. Faith in God and in his Son, Jesus Christ, is absolutely essential if we are to maintain a balanced perspective through times of trial and difficulty. While righteousness has never precluded adversity, faith in the Lord Jesus Christ can be a source of inner strength through which we may find comfort and the courage to cope.

I believe that each of us desires to be as courageous, noble, and steadfast as were Mary Fielding Smith and her son. What does that require? It requires us to follow this admonition from the book of Proverbs:

"Trust in the Lord with all thine heart; and lean not unto thine own understanding. In all thy ways acknowledge him, and he shall direct thy paths" (Proverbs 3:5–6). As I have studied this passage and pondered and prayed over it, I have been struck with the frequency of these words in our scriptures and our life stories: desire, faith, prayer, hope, patience, and love.

In the beginning of our quest to cultivate these values and virtues, we must have the desire to make them part of our lives and then pray with faith that it will happen. Paul taught that hope is the anchor to our souls, and with hope we can be filled with love and charity. Patience and courage are the natural offspring of all these magnificent qualities as we learn to bear our burdens with deep inner strength. That strength comes through letting the Lord work with us to share our burdens. Our testimonies will be deep and everlasting, fortified with the knowledge that with the Lord's help, we can do it!

———

See Barbara B. Ballard, "'Trust in the Lord with All Thy Heart,'" Ye Shall Bear Record of Me *(Salt Lake City: Deseret Book, 2002), 271.*

WORK OF THE HEART

Elaine L. Jack

Charity is work of the heart.

The Savior said that "the great commandment in the law" is "Thou shalt love the Lord thy God with all thy heart, and with all thy soul, and with all thy mind" (Matthew 22:36–37). When we love the Lord with all our mind, soul, and heart, we love others. And charity abounds.

This isn't news to you, because you spend your days doing good for others—for your family, your neighbors, your sisters, even strangers. Your efforts to assist and help others have become so much a part of your personal style that, for the most part, they are spontaneous, instinctive, immediate.

Elaine L. Jack has served as general president of the Relief Society and as matron of the Cardston Alberta Temple. A native of Canada, she attended the University of Utah as an English major. She and her husband, Joseph E. Jack, are the parents of four sons.

You may think I am describing someone else. You may be saying, "There's nothing special about me. I'm just ordinary."

I'd say the same thing: "I'm just an ordinary woman with the same joys and frustrations of every other woman." Sometimes the frustrations are great, and sometimes the joys simple, like having an even number of socks come out of the dryer. We all work at feeling joy and finding peace. One of our greatest tools in the process is charity.

In the scriptures, we find many examples of women whose daily efforts reflected charity. With their hearts filled with the pure love of Christ, they responded to needs quickly and effectively.

Rebekah, who eventually became the wife of Isaac and the mother of Jacob and Esau, was just such a woman. In the normal pattern of her daily tasks, she was kind to Abraham's servant who was visiting her village on the dramatic mission to secure a wife for Isaac.

The Lord knew Rebekah's heart; he knew how she would respond when she observed a need. He answered the servant's prayer that the young woman who was to become Isaac's wife would offer him water.

In Genesis we read, "Behold, Rebekah came out . . . with her pitcher upon her shoulder" and went down to the well (Genesis

24:15). You know that story. The servant asked for a drink. Whole family trees hung in the balance of her answer.

She said, "Drink, my lord," and then added, "I will draw water for thy camels also, until they have done drinking.

"And she hasted, and emptied her pitcher into the trough, and ran again unto the well to draw water, and drew for all his camels" (Genesis 24:18–20).

Her brother Laban invited him to lodge, and not until the servant was introduced did she discover he was the servant of her uncle. Her charitable response to this stranger was automatic. She did not stop to think, *I am giving service,* nor did she consider the station of the one in need. She hastened to serve water—to camels.

Respectfully, she offered an act of service, a simple one, and from that act was born a family of great influence for whole dispensations. Rebekah loved with worthiness and willingness as a daughter of God. Remember the question, Who can gauge the reach of our goodness?

From her we learn that charity, though often quantified as the action, is actually the state of the heart that prompts us to love one another. She offered water. It was in the offering that charity was manifest.

Alma emphasized the importance of "having the love of God always in your hearts" (Alma 13:29). Charity is that love. Charity is a gift of the Spirit, for "all things which are good cometh of God" (Moroni 7:12). And this gift is multiplied as it is used.

Both the giver and the receiver are blessed. For charity purifies and sanctifies all it touches, and "whoso is found possessed of it at the last day, it shall be well with him" (Moroni 7:47).

The greatest acts of charity come from giving of yourself and receiving expressions of charity with humility as well. President Spencer W. Kimball illustrated this truth in an inspiring example. He said: "[The Savior's] gifts were rare ones: eyes to the blind, ears to the deaf, and legs to the lame; cleanliness to the unclean, wholeness to the infirm, and breath to the lifeless. His gifts were . . . forgiveness to the repentant, hope to the despairing. His friends gave him shelter, food, and love. He gave them of himself, his love, his service, his life. . . . We should strive to give as he gave. To give of oneself is a holy gift" (*The Wondrous Gift* [Salt Lake City: Deseret Book, 1978], 2).

I've thought about this: "To give of oneself is a holy gift." "We should strive to give as he gave." What wise counsel! When we give our time, our energy, our commitment, our testimony to others, we are giving of ourselves. We are sharing intangibles not easily left on the doorstep but easily deposited in the heart.

See Elaine L. Jack, "Strengthened in Charity," Ensign, November 1996, 91.

WOMEN OF CHARITY

Sheri Dew

I once attended a fireside where a General Authority began by asking the question, "How can you tell if someone is converted to Jesus Christ?" We gave dozens of answers about service and commitment and obedience, none of which satisfied him. Finally he said that while our comments were all good, he believed that the one sure measure of a person's conversion was how he or she treated others.

Frankly, I expected something more profound, but his assertion so intrigued me that it drove me to the scriptures, where after much study I began to see how profound his message was: When we turn our hearts to the Lord, we instinctively open our hearts to others.

After Alma the Younger was converted, his thoughts turned

Sheri Dew has served as second counselor in the Relief Society general presidency. A graduate of Brigham Young University in history and a best-selling author, she serves as president of Deseret Book Company.

immediately to his people, for he "could not bear that any human soul should perish" (Mosiah 28:3). After Enos's all-night conversion, he "began to feel a desire for the welfare of [his] brethren . . . ; wherefore, [he] did pour out [his] whole soul unto God for them" (Enos 1:9). The Savior taught Peter, simply: "When thou art converted, strengthen thy brethren" (Luke 22:32).

Almost every major scriptural sermon focuses on the way we treat each other. We are taught to turn the other cheek (Matthew 5:39), to be reconciled to each other (Matthew 5:24), to love our enemies and pray for those who despitefully use us (Matthew 5:44), to serve each other and avoid contention (Mosiah 2: 17, 32). Said Joseph Smith, "The nearer we get to our heavenly Father, the more we are disposed to look with compassion on perishing souls." He also said that "it is natural for females to have feelings of charity" (*History of The Church of Jesus Christ of Latter-day Saints*, ed. B. H. Roberts, 2d ed. rev., 7 vols. [Salt Lake City: The Church of Jesus Christ of Latter-day Saints, 1932–51], 5:24; 4:605).

Knowing this, Lucifer works hard at undermining our divine gift. All too often we fall into traps he has designed to estrange us from each other. He delights when we gossip and criticize and judge, when we stew over perceived offenses or measure ourselves against each other, or when we succumb to such envy that we even begrudge each other's successes. All of these spiritually debilitating behaviors wreak havoc in relationships. Let us not forget that Satan resents any righteous relationship—because he will never have even one. Thus his never-ending efforts to alienate us from one another.

A while ago a woman approached me after a fireside and asked, "Don't you feel guilty for choosing a career over marriage?" Her words hurt. But I'm sure her comment would have been different if she had known my heart, or if she had known how much time I've spent fasting and pleading with the Lord in the temple, seeking to understand His will for me. Only He knows how painful this process has been. But He also knows how grateful I am for the process, because it has sealed my heart to Him.

How often have you and I made judgments that are equally unfair? Why can't we resist the urge to second-guess and evaluate each other? Why do we judge everything from the way we keep house to how many children we do or do not have? Sometimes I wonder if the final judgment will be a breeze compared with what we've put each other through here on earth!

It is simply not for us to judge each other. The Lord has reserved that right for Himself, because only He knows our hearts and understands the varying circumstances of our lives. Principles and covenants are the same for all of us. But the application of those principles will differ from woman to woman. What we can do is encourage each other to constantly seek the direction of the Holy Ghost to help us make decisions and then to bless us with the reassurance that our lives are on course. Only when the Lord is directing our lives may we expect to feel peace about our choices. And His approval is so much more vital than that of the ward busybody.

Another kind of judging is more subtle but equally destructive. How often do we describe a sister with words like these: She's a convert. She's been inactive. She's a Utah Mormon. She's single. She's a stay-at-home mom.

When we label one another, we make judgments that divide us from each other and inevitably alienate us from the Lord. We gain nothing by segregating ourselves based on superficial differences. What we have in common—particularly our commitment to the same glorious cause—is so much more significant than any distinctions in our individual lives. We are our sister's keeper. Heaven forbid that we would ever make even one sister feel left out. If there is anyplace in all the world where a woman should feel that she belongs, it is in this Church.

None of us needs one more person pointing out where we've fallen short. What we do need are each other's compassion, prayers, and support. What if we were to decide today that we would make just one assumption about each other—that we are each doing the best we can? And what if we were to try a little harder to help each other? Imagine the cumulative effect, not to mention the effect on us spiritually. Followers of Christ who pray with all the energy of their hearts to be filled with his love, the pure love of Christ, will become like Him (Moroni 7:48). As we are filled with this love, we no longer feel envy or think evil of others. That's because "charity never faileth" (Moroni 7:46). Charity is demonstrated when we give someone the benefit of the doubt, or readily accept an apology, or refuse to pass along a juicy piece of gossip. Might we in prayer contemplate grudges we need to put behind us, jealousies we should let go, and relationships we could improve by simply laying our pride aside?

Said President Gordon B. Hinckley: "Do you want to be happy? Forget yourself and get lost in this great cause. Lend your efforts to helping people. . . . Work to lift and serve His sons and daughters. You will come to know a happiness that you have never known before. . . . Let's get the cankering, selfish attitude out of our lives . . . and stand a little taller . . . in the service of others" (*Teachings of Gordon B. Hinckley* [Salt Lake City: Deseret Book, 1997], 597).

Let us keep in mind Lucy Mack Smith's classic statement

that "we must cherish one another, watch over one another, [and] comfort one another . . . that we may all sit down in heaven together"? (quoted in *Teachings of Gordon B. Hinckley*, 545). There isn't anything righteous we can't accomplish if we will stand together.

See Sheri Dew, "Shall We Not Go Forward in So Great a Cause?" Arise and Shine Forth (Salt Lake City: Deseret Book, 2001), 21.

THE ROYAL LAW OF LOVE

Marion D. Hanks

I speak of the second commandment, linked inseparably by the Lord Jesus Christ with the "first and great commandment," being indeed "like unto it." Christ said, "On these two commandments hang all the law and the prophets" (Matthew 22:38–40).

The apostle James called the second commandment the "royal law" (James 2:8). Paul wrote to the Corinthians that "all the law is fulfilled in one word, even in this; Thou shalt love thy neighbour as thyself" (Galatians 5:14).

Christ's ministry and his teachings leave no room to doubt with what seriousness we must accept and apply this sacred instruction. As he taught the law of love, Jesus was asked, "And

Marion D. Hanks has served as a member of the First Quorum of the Seventy and as president of the British Mission. He and his wife, Maxine, served as president and matron of the Salt Lake Temple. They are the parents of five children.

who is my neighbour?" (Luke 10:29). In answer he told the story of a man traveling from Jerusalem to Jericho who fell among thieves and was robbed and wounded and left at the wayside half dead. A priest and a Levite came by and "looked on him, and passed by on the other side" (Luke 10:32; see also Luke 10:31).

Into this scene came a Samaritan, a man to whose people and cities the Twelve had been forbidden to go (Matthew 10:5–6), and he stopped and gave immediate and continuing aid to the troubled man. Jesus said: "Which now of these three, thinkest thou, was neighbour unto him that fell among the thieves?

"And he said, He that shewed mercy on him. Then said Jesus unto him, Go, and do thou likewise" (Luke 10:36–37).

Can there be any question as to the meaning of that story?

It would be difficult to find anyone offering resistance in principle to the virtue of giving service to others, yet there may be some who do not understand the place of vital importance in the fundamentals of our faith that Jesus gave it. For him, in his life and teachings, it was not an option. Indeed, he declared that without it one could not qualify for the greatest of eternal blessings—eternal life (Matthew 25:31–46). The scriptures consistently so teach—acts of Christian service are expressions of Christian love. My observation and experience confirm the truth of it for me.

Religion is not a thing apart from life. It is not principles and ordinances or missionary work or leadership as an end in themselves. It is manifested by the kind of people we are, by our relationship with our Heavenly Father and his Son and all of the commandments, by the measure in which we qualify for the approval of our own Spirit-guided conscience, and by the way we treat other people.

Our religion, centering in the life and mission of the Lord Jesus Christ, helps us comprehend that. God and Christ love us with a mature, perfect love. The plan by which they lead requires mortal instruments of their love. We have the great honor to be invited to be such instruments. We need them, but they also need us. In this service we find the roots of most of those blessings that God wants us to enjoy.

Once I was invited by a civic organization to present an award of recognition to the person who had done the most to help handicapped people in the area. When the honored lady, who was herself severely handicapped, came to the podium to receive her award, she walked between two stalwart men assisting her, with another wheeling an oxygen tank on a carrier behind her, helping her to breathe.

She protested her unworthiness but accepted the award on behalf of all others who had been helpful to the handicapped. She told how her saintly father had prepared her for her first day at school and then left his office to come home to meet her when she returned. He had prepared her to expect some disagreeable comments from a few who could not handle her physical appearance—the humped back and other problems. These birth defects, he had assured her, were no one's fault—they were the consequence of problems not yet solved in this imperfect and sometimes unfair world. "But," said he, "if you will always be more fair and more kind to others than a few of them may sometimes be to you, you will enjoy every sweet blessing life affords."

That was her one qualification, she said: she had tried to be more fair and more kind to others than a few of them had sometimes been to her.

The sweetness of true Christian service is often experienced in obscurity—in quiet rooms in homes and hospitals and places of confinement, in military barracks and refugee camps, and in other places far from public attention. Usually it is unheralded, but it reflects the standard set by the Savior for those who will "inherit the kingdom prepared . . . from the foundation of the world" (Matthew 25:34). These are they who serve the hungry and the thirsty and the naked and the homeless and those who are sick or imprisoned, and who do this after the pattern and in the spirit of him who said, "Inasmuch as ye have done it unto one of the least of these my brethren, ye have done it unto me" (Matthew 25:40).

To those who so serve, he promised eternal life (Matthew 25:46), while to those who fail to minister to the needy he said, "Inasmuch as ye did it not to one of the least of these, ye did it not to me" (Matthew 25:45).

The royal law of love is of sacred significance in the Lord's program for his people—an element as vital as any other in the gospel. It is inseparable from them and the spirit of them. It is well known to us institutionally; indeed, the Church to which we have the honor to belong is celebrated for knowing and acting upon it on occasions of great need across the earth.

———

See Marion D. Hanks, "The Royal Law of Love," Ensign, November 1988, 62.

Part Three

We Increase Our
Testimonies of
Jesus Christ

Spiritually Prepared

Barbara W. Winder

Qualities of spirituality do not come without effort. Like any other talent with which we are blessed, they must be constantly practiced. A famous pianist once said, "If I fail to practice for one day, I can tell the difference in my playing. If I fail to practice for two days, my family can tell the difference. If I fail for three days, the whole world can tell the difference." This same principle applies to us in our quest for exaltation.

In applying the parable of the ten virgins to our lives, our modern prophets have explained that the oil of preparation is accumulated drop by drop through daily righteous living.

Consistently attending sacrament meetings adds oil to our lamps. So too will fasting, praying individually and as a family,

---

Barbara Woodhead Winder has served as Relief Society general president and as a companion to her husband, Richard W. Winder, while he presided over the Czechoslovakia Prague Mission. They have served together as president and matron of the Nauvoo Illinois Temple.

visiting teaching, controlling our bodily appetites, teaching gospel principles, nourishing and nurturing, watching over one another, studying the scriptures, keeping the commandments. Each act of dedication and obedience is a drop of oil with which we can refuel our lamps. Keeping the commandments and following the words of the prophet may be the greatest preparation we can make for any eventuality to come.

Often the advice that is given by our prophets is so simple and practical that we overlook it and fail to heed it.

President Ezra Taft Benson has declared, "When we put God first, all other things fall into their proper place or drop out of our lives. Our love of the Lord will govern the claims for our affection, the demands on our time, the interests we pursue, and the order of our priorities" ("The Great Commandment—Love the Lord," *Ensign,* May 1988, 4).

We need to put God first and balance our spiritual and temporal preparations, that we might become virtuous women, righteous daughters, instruments in his hands to help prepare the way for his coming.

See Barbara W. Winder, "Becoming a Prepared People," Ensign, *November 1988, 88.*

PRAY WITH PURPOSE

~~~~~~

Ardeth G. Kapp

Some years ago when I was called to serve as the Young Women general president, I was searching for answers, for direction, for revelation, for comfort. I didn't just desire, I yearned to know more than I had ever known before about the way to pray more effectively and listen more intensely. I wanted to know how to pray with greater faith and how to hear the voice of the Lord in my mind and heart through the Holy Ghost. I am not suggesting we need a calling in the Church before we pray mightily to our Father in Heaven, but I know that when we do, guidance will come. Guidance at that time came for me while "feasting on the word." In Alma's guidance to his son Helaman, notice how this scripture attends to our actions, our thoughts, and our feelings: "Cry unto God for all thy support; yea, let all

————

Ardeth Greene Kapp has served as general president of Young Women. A popular teacher, speaker, and writer, she and her husband, Heber B. Kapp, have served as matron and president of the Cardston Alberta Temple.

thy doings be unto the Lord, and whithersoever thou goest let it be in the Lord; yea, let all thy thoughts be directed unto the Lord; yea, let the affections of thy heart be placed upon the Lord forever." And if that isn't enough, he continues, "Counsel with the Lord in all thy doings, and he will direct thee for good; yea, when thou liest down at night lie down unto the Lord, that he may watch over you in your sleep; and when thou risest in the morning let thy heart be full of thanks unto God; and if ye do these things, ye shall be lifted up at the last day" (Alma 37:36–37).

The answers do not usually come all at once, but a reminder of the availability of our Father in Heaven was the reassurance I needed at that time.

When we pray with purpose, there is power in prayer. President Gordon B. Hinckley tells us, "Members can fight evil with prayer." Hear his words, "Believe in getting on your knees every morning and every night and talking to your Father in Heaven concerning the feelings of your hearts and the desires of your minds in righteousness. Believe in prayer, there is nothing like it. When all is said and done there is no power on earth like the power of prayer" (*Church News*, 29 January 2000).

In answer to our prayers, our Father in Heaven will open doors for us, soften hearts, heal wounds, spiritual and physical, and just make things better all around. He wants us to be good, and he wants us to be happy. On occasion, we will realize that we have been allowed to participate in the answer to someone else's prayer.

———

See Ardeth G. Kapp, "Pressing Forward," Arise and Shine Forth (Salt Lake City: Deseret Book, 2001), 35.

In Times of Crisis

Janette Hales Beckham

You may have read the book *The Hiding Place,* by Corrie ten Boom. The scriptures were an answer for her in a time much more bleak than most of us will ever have to face.

Corrie and her sister, Betsy, lived Christian lives in prewar Holland. They responded to the brutality against Jewish people by hiding them in the family home. When the hiding place was discovered, the sisters were shipped to a death camp, where they suffered all the deprivation heaped upon the Jewish prisoners.

In an unusual way, Corrie was able to keep a Bible. She led scripture readings with the other prisoners. Their outer world of suffering grew "harder and harder." But she described their inner life as just the opposite. In her words:

"Our Bible was the center of an ever-widening circle of help

Janette Hales Beckham has served as general president of Young Women. She and her late husband, Robert H. Hales, became the parents of five children. She married Raymond E. Beckham in 1995.

and hope. Like waifs clustered around a blazing fire, we gathered about it, holding out our hearts to its warmth and light. The blacker the night around us grew, the brighter and truer and more beautiful burned the word of God. . . .

"Life . . . took place on two separate levels. One, the observable, external life, grew every day more horrible. The other, the life we lived with God, grew daily better, truth upon truth, glory upon glory" (*The Hiding Place* [New York City: Bantam Books, 1974], 194–95).

Others have testified of the power of the scriptures. In knowing the scriptures and trusting our Heavenly Father's words, our Savior himself was an example to us. It is recorded in the fourth chapter of Luke that when Jesus had fasted for forty days and was tempted by the devil, the devil suggested that if Jesus were the Son of God, he turn a stone into bread. Even after fasting forty days, Jesus said, "Man shall not live by bread alone, but by every word of God" (Luke 4:4). Jesus knew the words of the prophets.

Satan again tempted Jesus, offering him power and glory if he would worship Satan. Jesus resisted the temptation and responded with the words, "It is written, Thou shalt worship the Lord thy God, and him only shalt thou serve" (Luke 4:8). Jesus knew his Father's will, and the words strengthened him in a time of temptation.

The words of the scriptures will strengthen us in times of temptation. The scriptures have been given to us to help us find peace and reassurance in times of crisis, to help us find solutions to our everyday challenges, to strengthen us in times of temptation. The scriptures will help us improve our behavior as we come to know our Savior, Jesus Christ.

———

See Janette C. Hales, "Ye Shall Feast upon This Fruit," Ensign, May 1995, 91.

DIVINE DIRECTIONS

～

L. Lionel Kendrick

When we left our heavenly home to take this trip through mortality, we received instructions and divine directions that would assist us in returning home safely to our Heavenly Father. These directions were clearly communicated to prepare us for our earthly experiences. The scriptures become a road map, a set of divine directions to assist us on our journey through mortality and our return trip home. Just as a road map not read, the scriptures not searched are of little value to us in providing directions.

Are we studying our divine directions daily? When was the last time we checked our celestial compass to see if we are still on course? The road to the celestial kingdom is one way. When we fail to search the scriptures, we may find ourselves going the wrong way on a one-way highway.

———

L. Lionel Kendrick, who has served as a member of the First Quorum of the Seventy, was converted to the Church while serving in the U.S. Air Force. He and his wife, Myrtis Lee Noble Kendrick, are the parents of four children.

Scriptures reveal the divine desires of the Lord in our behalf. Each of us should have a burning desire to search the scriptures diligently and daily to seek the will of the Lord in our life. For some it may be necessary to develop the discipline to search the scriptures daily.

One of the most sacred purposes for which the scriptures were written was to make it possible for all to know Christ. The scriptures teach and testify of Jesus Christ. They teach us much that we need to know and to do to return to the presence of the Savior. John was specific in giving the purpose of the scriptures when he said: "But these [things] are written, that ye might believe that Jesus is the Christ, the Son of God; and that believing ye might have life through his name" (John 20:31).

The Savior provided counsel as to the way we should study scripture. He said: "And now, whoso readeth, let him understand; he that hath the scriptures, let him search them" (3 Nephi 10:14). The Prophet Joseph Smith counseled:

"Search the scriptures—search the revelations . . . and ask your Heavenly Father, in the name of His Son Jesus Christ, to manifest the truth unto you, and if you do it with an eye single to His glory nothing doubting, He will answer you by the power of His Holy Spirit. You will then know for yourselves and not for another. You will not then be dependent on man for the knowledge of God; nor will there be any room for speculation" (*Teachings of the Prophet Joseph Smith,* sel. Joseph Fielding Smith [Salt Lake City: Deseret Book, 1978], 11–12).

It is not enough to read the scriptures. Random reading results in reduced retention. We must search for specifics. We must seek for truth and increased understanding of its application in our lives.

If we are to be effective in our study of the scriptures, we must prepare for it to be a special spiritual experience. The following suggestions may be helpful.

Schedule. Schedule a time to search the scriptures daily. Scripture study is such an essential part of our spiritual development that we must take time and make it a priority in our daily schedule. Our spirits should never be deprived of the much-needed spiritual nourishment which comes from scripture study. Without this spiritual food, our spirits become starved and weakened to temptation. President Spencer W. Kimball taught the principle that "no father, no son, no mother, no daughter should get so busy that he or she does not have time to study the scriptures and the words of modern prophets" ("Boys Need Heroes Close By," *Ensign,* May 1976, 47).

Pray. We should begin and end each study session with prayer. We must invite the Spirit to teach us. Nephi taught that "the mysteries of God shall be unfolded . . . by the power of the Holy Ghost" (1 Nephi 10:19).

Search. To search is to seek, to explore, to examine carefully. As we study, we should do so with purpose, searching for specifics and an expansion of our vision of eternal truth. We must search for principles, doctrines, answers to questions, and solutions to problems. We should look for doctrinal relationships and for possible hidden meanings of that which has been recorded.

Ponder. To ponder is to meditate, to think, to feast, and to treasure. It is more than a mental method; it is a spiritual striving to obtain and to understand truth. We should follow the process taught by the Savior to the Nephites as he taught them sacred principles. He then instructed them to "go ye unto your homes, and ponder upon the things which I have said, and ask of the Father, in my name, that ye may understand, and prepare your minds for the morrow" (3 Nephi 17:3). As we ponder, we should follow the counsel of the Savior when he said, "Treasure up in your minds continually the words of life" (D&C 84:85). This implies that we should repeat in our minds the principles we have learned and draw upon them in each of our decisions.

Relate. Nephi has counseled to "liken all scriptures unto us, that it might be for our profit and learning" (1 Nephi 19:23). We must read as if the Lord were speaking directly to us in a personal manner.

Apply. President Marion G. Romney counseled: "Learning the gospel from the written word . . . is not enough. It must also be lived. . . . One cannot fully learn the gospel without living it" ("Records of Great Worth," *Ensign,* September 1980, 4). As we learn a principle, we must make a real effort to apply and to live it in our life.

The scriptures are priceless possessions. If we search the scriptures, seeking for the plain and precious principles, the Lord will reveal his will unto us and we will be richly blessed. If we research the revelations and respond correctly to them, we will return home safely to Heavenly Father.

———

See L. Lionel Kendrick, "Search the Scriptures," Ensign, May 1993, 13.

THE KINGDOM OF GOD
IS WITHIN YOU

Patricia T. Holland

Often we fail to consider the glorious possibility within our own souls. We need to remember that divine promise, "The kingdom of God is within you" (Luke 17:21). Perhaps we forget that the kingdom of God is within us because too much attention is given to this outer shell, this human body of ours, and the frail, too-flimsy world in which it moves.

Permit me to share with you an analogy that I created from something I read years ago. It helped me then—and helps me still—in my examination of inner strength and spiritual growth.

The analogy is of a soul—a human soul, with all of its splendor—being placed in a beautifully carved but very tightly locked box. Reigning in majesty and illuminating our soul in this innermost box is our Lord and our Redeemer, Jesus Christ, the

Patricia Terry Holland has served as first counselor in the Young Women general presidency. She and her husband, Elder Jeffrey R. Holland of the Quorum of the Twelve Apostles, are the parents of three children.

living Son of the living God. This box is then placed—and locked—inside another, larger one, and so on until five beautifully carved but very securely locked boxes await the woman who is skillful and wise enough to open them. In order for her to have free communication with the Lord, she must find the key to and unlock the contents of these boxes. Success will then reveal to her the beauty and divinity of her own soul and her gifts and her grace as a daughter of God.

For me, *prayer* is the key to the first box. We kneel to ask help for our tasks and then arise to find that the first lock is now open. But this ought not to seem just a convenient and contrived miracle, for if we are to search for real light and eternal certainties, we have to pray as the ancients prayed. We are women now, not children, and we are expected to pray with maturity. The words most often used to describe urgent, prayerful labor are *wrestle, plead, cry,* and *hunger.* In some sense, prayer may be the hardest work we ever will engage in, and perhaps it should be. It is pivotal protection against becoming so involved with worldly possessions and honors and status that we no longer desire to undertake the search for our soul.

For those who, like Enos, pray in faith and gain entrance to a new dimension of their potential divinity, they are led to box number two. Here our prayers alone do not seem to be sufficient.

We must turn to the scriptures for God's long-recorded teachings about our souls. We must learn. Surely every woman in this church is under divine obligation to learn and grow and develop. We are God's diverse array of unburnished talents, and we must not bury these gifts or hide our light. If the glory of God is intelligence, then learning, especially learning from the scriptures, stretches us toward him.

He uses many metaphors for divine influence, such as "living water" (John 4:10) and the "bread of life" (John 6:35). I have discovered that if my own progress stalls, it stalls from malnutrition born of failing to eat and drink daily from his holy writ. There have been challenges in my life that would have completely destroyed me had I not had the scriptures both on my bedstand and in my purse so that I could partake of them day and night at a moment's notice. Meeting God in scripture has been like a divine intravenous feeding for me—a celestial IV that my son once described as an *angelical* cord. So box two is opened through *learning from the scriptures*. I have discovered that by studying them I can have, again and again, an exhilarating encounter with God.

At the beginning of such success in emancipating the soul, however, Lucifer becomes more anxious, especially as we approach box number three. He knows that we are about to learn one very important and fundamental principle—that to truly find ourselves we must lose ourselves—so he begins to block our increased efforts to love God, our neighbor, and ourselves. Through the past several decades, Satan has enticed all humanity to engage almost all of their energies in the pursuit of romantic love or thing-love or excessive self-love. In so doing, we forget that appropriate self-love and self-esteem are the promised reward for putting others first. "Whosoever shall seek to save his life shall lose it; and whosoever shall lose his life shall preserve it" (Luke 17:33). Box three opens only to the key of *charity.*

With charity, real growth and genuine insight begin. But the lid to box four seems nearly impossible to penetrate. Unfortunately, the faint-hearted and fearful often turn back here. The going seems too difficult, the lock too secure. This is a time for self-evaluation. To see ourselves as we really are often brings pain, but it is only through true humility, repentance, and renewal that we will come to know God. "Learn of me; for I am meek and lowly in heart," he said (Matthew 11:29). We must be patient with ourselves as we overcome weaknesses, and we must remember to rejoice over all that is good in us. This will strengthen our inner selves and leave us less dependent on outward acclaim. When our souls pay less attention to public praise, they then also care very little about public disapproval. Competition and jealousy and envy now begin to have no meaning. Just imagine the powerful spirit that would exist in our female society if we finally arrived at the point where, like our Savior, our real desire was to be counted as the *least* among our sisters. The rewards here are of such profound strength and quiet triumph of faith that we are carried into an even brighter sphere. So the fourth box, unlike the others, is broken open, just as a contrite heart is broken. *We are reborn*—like a flower growing and blooming out of the broken crust of the earth.

To share with you my feelings of opening the fifth box, I must compare the beauty of our souls with the holiness of our temples. There, in a setting not of this world, where fashions and position and professions go unrecognized, we have our chance to find peace and serenity and stillness that will anchor our soul forever, for there we may find God. For those of us who, like the brother of Jared, have the courage and faith to break through the veil into that sacred center of existence (Ether 3:6–19), we will find the brightness of the final box brighter than the noonday sun. There we find wholeness—holiness. That is what it says over the entrance to the fifth box: *Holiness to the Lord.* "Know ye not that ye are the temple of God?" (1 Corinthians 3:16). I testify that you are holy—that divinity is abiding within you waiting to be uncovered—to be unleashed and magnified and demonstrated.

As women, all of us are Eve's daughters, whether we are married or single, maternal or barren. We are created in the image of

God to become gods and goddesses. And we can provide something of that divine pattern, that maternal prototype, for each other and for those who come after us. Whatever our circumstances, we can reach out, touch, hold, lift, and nurture—but we cannot do it in isolation. We need a community of sisters stilling the soul and binding the wounds of fragmentation.

———

See Patricia T. Holland, "'One Thing Needful': Becoming Women of Greater Faith in Christ," Ensign, *October 1987, 26.*

Part Four

We Follow
the Promptings
of the Holy Ghost

OUR SPIRITUAL EDGE

Howard W. Hunter

All of us face times in our lives when we need heavenly help in a special and urgent way. We all have moments when we are overwhelmed by circumstances or confused by the counsel we get from others, and we feel a great need to receive spiritual guidance, a great need to find the right path and do the right thing. In the scriptural preface to this latter-day dispensation, the Lord promised that if we would be humble in such times of need and turn to him for aid, we would "be made strong, and [be] blessed from on high, and receive knowledge from time to time" (D&C 1:28). That help is ours if we will but seek it, trust in it, and follow what

Howard W. Hunter was ordained an apostle by David O. McKay in 1959 and sustained president of the Church in 1994. He and Claire Jeffs were married in the Salt Lake Temple in 1931 and became the parents of three children. After her death, he married Inis Bernice Egan. President Hunter died in 1995 at the age of eighty-seven.

King Benjamin, in the Book of Mormon, called "the enticings of the Holy Spirit" (Mosiah 3:19).

Perhaps no promise in life is more reassuring than that promise of divine assistance and spiritual guidance in times of need. It is a gift freely given from heaven, a gift that we need from our earliest youth through the very latest days of our lives.

Sometimes we may feel that our spiritual edge has grown dull. On some very trying days, we may even feel that God has forgotten us, has left us alone in our confusion and concern. But that feeling is no more justified for the older ones among us than it is for the younger and less experienced. God knows and loves us all. We are, every one of us, his daughters and his sons, and whatever life's lessons may have brought us, the promise is still true: "If any of you lack wisdom, let him ask of God, that giveth to all men liberally, and upbraideth not; and it shall be given him" (James 1:5).

There may be so very much our Father in Heaven would like to give us—young, old, or middle-aged—if we would but seek his presence regularly through such avenues as scripture study and earnest prayer. Of course, developing spirituality and attuning ourselves to the highest influences of godliness is not an easy matter. It takes time and frequently involves a struggle.

Elisha, a prophet, seer, and revelator, had counseled the king of Israel on how and where and when to defend against the warring Syrians. The king of Syria, of course, wished to rid his army of Elisha's prophetic interference. The record reads:

"Therefore sent he thither horses, and chariots, and a great host: and they came by night, and compassed the city about. . . .

"[They] compassed the city both with horses and chariots" (2 Kings 6:14–15).

The odds were staggering. It was an old man and a boy against what looked like the whole world. Elisha's young companion was fearful and cried, "Alas, my master! how shall we do?" And Elisha's reply? "Fear not: for they that be with us are more than they that be with them" (2 Kings 6:15–16). But there were no others with the old man and his young companion. From what source could their help possibly come?

Then Elisha turned his eyes heavenward, saying, "Lord, I pray thee, open his eyes, that he may see." And, we read, "the Lord opened the eyes of the young man; and he saw: and, behold, the mountain was full of horses and chariots of fire round about Elisha" (2 Kings 6:17).

In the gospel of Jesus Christ, we have help from on high. "Be of good cheer," the Lord says, "for I will lead you along" (D&C 78:18). "I will impart unto you of my Spirit, which shall enlighten your mind, which shall fill your soul with joy" (D&C 11:13).

I testify of the divinity of Jesus Christ. God does live, and he imparts to us his Spirit. In facing life's problems and meeting life's tasks, may we all claim that gift from God, our Father, and find spiritual joy.

———

See Howard W. Hunter, "Blessed from on High," Ensign, November 1988, 59.

The Lord, His Mouthpiece, and the Holy Ghost

Virginia H. Pearce

We have a son and sons-in-law who love to golf, so you can imagine their excitement when they had an opportunity to attend a golf clinic with a world-famous pro.

Reporting the highlight of the day, our son said: "The pro slowly went from person to person. He watched each person swing and then gave suggestions. When he came to me, he said: 'Basically, you've got a very good swing. Now this time, when you swing back, extend a little further to the right and explode through. Good,' he said. 'Practice that way. And if anyone ever tries to tell you differently, you tell them that I said you have a great swing!' Then he moved on to the next golfer, and I kept practicing."

Virginia H. Pearce, who received a master's degree in social work from the University of Utah, has served as first counselor in the Young Women general presidency. She and her husband, James R. Pearce, are the parents of six children.

"Did it work?" we asked.

"Not yet, but it will," he answered confidently.

As the boys went on through the room and out the other door to do a little more practicing in the backyard, I felt a twinge of envy. Wouldn't it be nice if there were someone whom I trusted that much—an expert who could take a look at my life and say: "Basically, you're doing great. But if you would just do this one little thing, it would make a big difference"?

Maybe you have been to those late-night parties with girl-friends where they all decide to tell what's wrong with you! Not something I would recommend. That kind of an experience just leaves everyone feeling bad. No, I want my information from a real expert.

All at once, the light turned on! General conference! No won-der I look forward to those meetings and messages! Here are my experts: the prophets who reassure me that basically my swing is good and then give instructions about what I should do or should stop doing that will make a big difference. Not only are these men experienced but their instructions come directly from Heavenly Father to me by way of the Holy Ghost—personalized to my exact, immediate, and individual needs. Who could be trusted more than this combination: the Lord, his mouthpiece, and the Holy Ghost?

Listen to and read the words of President Gordon B. Hinckley. It's easy to say: "That was a really good talk. He's one of my favorite speakers." Then we go home and continue to be the same people with the same problems. President Hinckley and other General Authorities will speak to us at the next general conference. Listen with new ears. Read and reread the messages. Is the Lord using his prophets to answer your prayers? Is the Lord using his prophets to send you a message that you are loved and are on the right road—that fundamentally your swing is great? Is the Lord using his prophets to give you some instructions to practice or warnings to act on?

Identify, with the help of the Holy Ghost, a personal message—the little corrections you should make in your swing. There will be an idea or a few words that you will feel are spoken just for you. Their interpretation will be yours alone. This is the process of personal revelation. It is simple. Don't brush it aside.

Put the message into action. Practice. "Be ye doers of the word, and not hearers only" (James 1:22). This is the whole point of revelation. It doesn't matter how often the Lord chooses to speak to us if we fail to do anything about it.

Don't be discouraged—keep trying until you succeed. We are entitled to the help of the Lord when we are trying to do his will. Pray for that help and keep trying.

Notice the changes in your life and feelings. Good feelings will come when we conform our lives to the will of God as expressed through his chosen prophets.

President Hinckley has asked us to "try a little harder to be a little better" ("We Have a Work to Do," *Ensign*, May 1995, 88). I pray that we will follow that advice—that we will approach the messages of the prophet with an enthusiasm born of our desire to have the experts reinforce and instruct us in righteous living.

———

See Virginia H. Pearce, "Listening with New Ears," Ensign, *May 1996, 85.*

PEACE THROUGH PRAYER

Rex D. Pinegar

Our Father in Heaven has promised us peace in times of trial and has provided a way for us to come to him in our need. He has given us the privilege and power of prayer. He has told us to "pray always" and has promised he will pour out his Spirit upon us (D&C 19:38).

Thankfully, we can call upon him anytime, anywhere. We can speak to him in the quiet thoughts of our mind and from the deepest feelings of our heart. It has been said, "Prayer is made up of heart throbs and the righteous yearnings of the soul" (James E. Talmage, *Jesus the Christ* [Salt Lake City: Deseret Book, 1977], 238).

Our Heavenly Father has told us he knows our thoughts and the intents of our hearts (D&C 6:16). This power enables us to

Rex D. Pinegar has served as a member of the First Quorum of the Seventy and as a member of the presidency of the Seventy. He and his wife, Bonnie Lee Crabb, are the parents of six children.

81

go beyond the limits of our verbal language to the understanding of our thoughts, our true needs and desires.

President Marion G. Romney taught: "Sometimes the Lord puts thoughts in our minds in answer to prayers. . . . [He] gives us peace in our minds" (Conference Report, Taiwan Area Conference, 1975, 7). For example, in response to Oliver Cowdery's prayer to know if the translation of the plates by Joseph Smith was true, the Lord answered, "Did I not speak peace to your mind concerning the matter? What greater witness can you have than from God?" (D&C 6:23).

The peace God speaks to our minds will let us know when decisions we have made are right, when our course is true.

It can come as personal inspiration and guidance to assist us in our daily life—in our homes, in our work. It can provide us with courage and hope to meet the challenges of life. The miracle of prayer, to me, is that in the private, quiet chambers of our mind and heart, God both hears *and* answers prayers.

Perhaps the greatest test of our faith and the most difficult part of prayer may be to recognize the answer that comes to us in a thought or a feeling and then to accept or to act on the answer God chooses to give. Consistency in prayer, along with searching the scriptures and following the counsel of living prophets, keeps us in tune with the Lord and enables us to interpret the promptings of the Spirit more easily. The Lord has said, "Learn of me, and listen to my words; walk in the meekness of my Spirit, and you shall have peace in me" (D&C 19:23).

There is terrible suffering in our world today. Tragic things happen to good people. God does not cause them, nor does he always prevent them. He does, however, strengthen us and bless us with his peace, through earnest prayer.

"It is not the usual purpose of prayer to serve us like Aladdin's lamp, to bring us ease without effort," Elder Richard L. Evans wrote. "Prayer is not a matter of asking only. It should not be always as the beggar's upturned hand. Often the purpose of prayer is to give us strength to do what needs to be done, wisdom to see the way to solve our own problems, and ability to do our best in our tasks. We need to pray . . . for strength to endure, for faith and fortitude to face what sometimes must be faced" (*The Man and the Message* [Salt Lake City: Bookcraft, 1973], 289).

Sometimes, when our prayers are not answered as we desire, we may feel the Lord has rejected us or that our prayer was in vain. We may begin to doubt our worthiness before God, or even the reality and power of prayer. That is when we must continue to pray with patience and faith and to listen for that peace.

———————

See Rex D. Pinegar, "Peace through Prayer," Ensign, May 1993, 65.

THE VOICE IS STILL SMALL

Graham W. Doxey

President Spencer W. Kimball said: "The burning bushes, the smoking mountains, . . . the Cumorahs, and the Kirtlands were realities; but they were the exceptions. The great volume of revelation came to Moses and to Joseph and comes to today's prophet in the less spectacular way—that of deep impressions, without spectacle or glamour or dramatic events. Always expecting the spectacular, many will miss entirely the constant flow of revealed communication" (Conference Report, Munich Germany Area Conference, 1973, 77).

Dramatic and miraculous answers to prayer may come, but they are the exceptions. Even at the highest levels of responsibility in this kingdom of God, which is being built up upon the earth, *the voice is still small.*

Graham Watson Doxey has served as a member of the Second Quorum of the Seventy and as president of the Missouri Independence Mission. He and his wife, Mary Lou Young Doxey, are the parents of twelve children.

In the Bible we read of the account of an earlier prophet who was rejected and discouraged. The word of the Lord came to Elijah when the children of Israel had forsaken their covenant and thrown down altars and slain prophets. He was told to "go forth, and stand upon the mount before the Lord. And, behold, the Lord passed by, and a great and strong wind rent the mountains, and brake in pieces the rocks before the Lord; but the Lord was not in the wind: and after the wind an earthquake; but the Lord was not in the earthquake:

"And after the earthquake a fire; but the Lord was not in the fire: and after the fire a still small voice" (1 Kings 19:11–12).

Listening is a challenge for us all today.

Time to listen. The *ability* to listen. The *desire* to listen. On religious matters, too many of us are saying, "What did you say? Speak up; I can't hear you." And when he doesn't *shout* back, or cause the bush to burn, or write us a message in stone with his finger, we are inclined to think he doesn't listen, doesn't care about us. Some even conclude there is no God.

"Aids to our hearing" are available. How can we filter out the heavy decibels of darkness that surround us? Let me mention three of the more obvious ones.

Number 1: Revitalize your weekly worship. When you sing the hymns, for instance, ponder the meaning of the words, enjoy the spirit of the music. Sing with enthusiasm without regard to your tones. You will have a good feeling, and your spirit will be enlivened; and as you join with the Saints in the songs of the heart, the Lord promises to answer this with blessings upon your head (D&C 25:12).

Next, *partake* of the sacrament. Don't merely *take* the sacrament. Think of the covenants you are remaking. Truly witness unto the Father that you will take upon yourself the name of his Son, even Jesus Christ. Recommit yourself to always remember him, to keep the commandments which he has given you. Your obedience will entitle you to have his Spirit to be with you. If this sacred ordinance has become commonplace in your worship, if you let your mind wander elsewhere during this weekly opportunity for spiritual renewal, if you just *take* the bread and water as it passes, with no thought or recommitment in your life, then you have turned off a significant aid to your hearing.

Number 2: Pray to know God's will, not to "get things." Too often, because of our selfish desires, after a cursory "Thank you, Lord," we consume our prayer time in the listing of things we want, even of things we think we need. We must be willing to release the death grip which we have on things, which have become as a security blanket in our lives. Count the many hundreds of needed missionary couples who would be serving in the field if that firm grip on the familiarities of home and of children and grandchildren could be loosened. The Lord is prepared to perform the miracle that will follow, which miracle is that both they and you will survive, even grow, with an eighteen-month separation. We must learn to pray with meaning, "Not my will, but Thy will be done." When you are able to do this, his whisperings to you will be loud and clear.

Hearing aid number 3 has to do with the scriptures. In the Doctrine and Covenants the Lord tells us that he speaks to us through the scriptures. Of course, just reading words without our minds being centered on the message is not really listening. In section 18 we read:

"And I, Jesus Christ, your Lord and your God, have spoken it.

"These words are not of men nor of man, but of me; wherefore, you shall testify they are of me and not of man:

"For it is my voice which speaketh them unto you; for they are given by my Spirit unto you, . . .

"Wherefore, you can testify that you have heard my voice, and know my words" (D&C 18:33–36).

And thus, what to many seems to be the monologue of prayer actually becomes a dialogue with God as we immerse ourselves in the scriptures.

As it was with Elijah, so it is today. God is not in the earthquake, nor in the winds and fires of war, but he speaks to us in a voice that is small.

———

See Graham W. Doxey, "The Voice Is Still Small," Ensign, November 1991, 25.

WE ARE NOT ALONE

Sheri Dew

Nephi taught: "If ye will . . . receive the Holy Ghost, it will show unto you all things what ye should do" (2 Nephi 32:5). What a remarkable privilege and promise! Lorenzo Snow said that it is the "grand privilege of every Latter-day Saint . . . to have the manifestations of the spirit every day of our lives . . . [so] that we may know the light, and not be groveling continually in the dark" (Conference Report, April 1899, 52). And his sister Eliza R. Snow declared: "You may talk to the [Saints] about the follies of the world . . . till dooms day, and it will make no impression. But . . . place them in a position where they will get the Holy Ghost, and that will be a sure protection against outside influences" (*Woman's Exponent,* 15 September 1873, 63). We have been promised the constant companionship of the third member of the

---

Sheri Dew has served as second counselor in the Relief Society general presidency. A graduate of Brigham Young University in history and a best-selling author, she serves as president of Deseret Book Company.

Godhead and hence the privilege of receiving revelation for our own lives. We are *not* alone!

The Holy Ghost enlarges our minds, our hearts, and our understanding; helps us subdue weaknesses and resist temptation; inspires humility and repentance; guides and protects us in miraculous ways; and gifts us with wisdom, divine encouragement, peace of mind, a desire to change, and the ability to differentiate between the philosophies of men and revealed truth. The Holy Ghost is the minister and messenger of the Father and the Son, and He testifies of Their glorious, global reality and Their connection to us personally. Without the presence of the Spirit, it is impossible to comprehend our personal mission or to have the reassurance that our course is right. No mortal comfort can duplicate that of the Comforter. Said President Hinckley, "There is *no greater blessing* that can come into our lives than . . . the companionship of the Holy Spirit" (Boston Massachusetts Regional Conference, 22 April 1995; italics added). And yet Brigham Young lamented: "[We] may have the Spirit of the Lord to . . . direct [us]. . . . I am satisfied, however, that, in this respect, we live far beneath our privileges" (*Deseret News Semi-Weekly,* 3 December 1867, 2).

Is it possible that in this twilight season of the dispensation of the fulness of times, when Satan and his minions roam the earth inspiring deceit, discouragement, and despair, that we who have been armed with the most potent antidote on earth—the gift of the Holy Ghost—don't always fully partake of that gift? Are we guilty of spiritually just "getting by" and not accessing the power and protection within our reach? Are we satisfied with far less than the Lord is willing to give us, essentially opting to go it alone here rather than partner with the Divine?

This Church is a church of revelation. Our challenge is not one of getting the Lord to speak to us. Our problem is hearing what He has to say. He has promised, "As often as thou hast inquired thou hast received instruction of my Spirit" (D&C 6:14).

It is vital that we, the sisters of Relief Society, learn to hear the voice of the Lord. Yet I worry that too often we fail to seek the guidance of the Spirit. Perhaps we don't know how and haven't made it a priority to learn. Or we're so aware of our personal failings that we don't feel worthy, don't really believe the Lord will talk to *us,* and therefore don't seek revelation. Or we've allowed the distractions and pace of our lives to crowd out the Spirit. What a tragedy! The Holy Ghost blesses us with optimism and wisdom at times of challenge that we simply cannot muster on our own. No wonder that one of the adversary's favorite tactics among righteous LDS women is busyness—getting us so preoccupied with the flurry of daily life that we fail to immerse ourselves in the gospel of Jesus Christ. Sisters, we can't afford *not* to seek the things of the Spirit! There is too much at stake. Too many people are depending on us as mothers, as sisters, leaders, and friends. A woman led by the Lord knows where to turn for answers and for peace. She can make difficult decisions and face problems with confidence because she takes her counsel from the Spirit and from her leaders who are also guided by the Spirit.

Our ability to hear spiritually is linked to our willingness to work at it. President Hinckley has often said that the only way he knows to get anything done is to get on his knees and plead for help and then get on his feet and go to work. That combination of faith and hard work is the consummate curriculum for learning the language of the Spirit. The Savior taught, "Blessed are all they who do *hunger* and *thirst* after righteousness, for they shall be filled with the Holy Ghost" (3 Nephi 12:6; italics added). Hungering and thirsting translate to sheer spiritual labor. Worshiping in the temple, repenting to become increasingly pure, forgiving and seeking forgiveness, and earnest fasting and prayer all increase our receptivity to the Spirit. Spiritual work *works* and is the key to learning to hear the voice of the Lord.

Elder Bruce R. McConkie said, "There is no price too high . . . no sacrifice too great, if out of it all we . . . enjoy the gift of the Holy Ghost" (*A New Witness for the Articles of Faith* [Salt

Lake City: Deseret Book, 1984], 253). What *are* we willing to do, what weaknesses and indulgences will we give up, to have as our personal protector and guide the constant companionship of the Holy Ghost?

It is a question worth asking, for let us be clear: The adversary *delights* in separating us, the sisters of this Church, from the Spirit because he knows how vital our influence and our presence are in the latter-day kingdom of God. It is the Holy Ghost who leads us to the Lord, who binds us to Him, and who irrevocably seals our testimony of Him.

———

See Sheri Dew, "We Are Not Alone," Ensign, November 1998, 94.

Part Five

We Dedicate Ourselves to Strengthening Marriages and Families

No Ordinary Battle

Ardeth G. Kapp

Today a battle is being waged, and it is no ordinary battle. The safety, the protection, the survival, the sanctity of the family are under attack as never before. The traditional family structure is disintegrating, and many individuals are suffering deep and serious wounds. There is an increasing number of casualties. Problems with crime, drugs, alcohol, immorality, abuse, and even suicide are growing at an alarming rate. This is no ordinary battle. The enemy is real, and the family is the target.

In the fight against the devastating influences that press upon even the most traditional and solid families, it is important to keep in mind the vision of where we ultimately want to be. An understanding of all that is past and the promises of the future

Ardeth Greene Kapp has served as general president of Young Women. A popular teacher, speaker, and writer, she and her husband, Heber B. Kapp, have served as matron and president of the Cardston Alberta Temple.

helps give us the vision to make daily decisions of eternal consequence. Without discernment or foresight to see beyond the urgencies or apparent crises of the moment, we can win the battle but lose the war.

In his infinite mercy, God has revealed to us a great vision concerning the family. The knowledge that God is our Father and we are his children places the family unit in the most exalted position. Think of it: We existed with him in a family relationship as his children! We were faithful, valiant, and obedient; and, despite the opposing forces there, we chose to keep our first estate and then to come to this mortal life knowing it would be a time of severe trials and testing.

We have been told that we will experience opposition in all things and learn to act for ourselves (2 Nephi 2:16). This mortal life provides the opportunities for us to qualify ourselves to become joint-heirs with Jesus Christ, to establish eternal family relationships through the sealing power of the priesthood, and to have eternal increase in the celestial kingdom.

With the vision of our next home, we can gain a better understanding of our existence here and the importance of our family relationships. The more aware we are that the spirit world is an extension of our mortal existence, the better prepared we are to set aside the treasures of this world and to establish priorities in relation to the next.

————

See Ardeth G. Kapp, My Neighbor, My Sister, My Friend *(Salt Lake City: Deseret Book, 1990), 101–3.*

An Everyday
and Every-Way Relationship

~

Marion D. Hanks

When the gospel was restored, there came a renewed understanding of temples and temple worship. The power to bind and seal on earth and in heaven has again been entrusted to authorized servants of God. Eternal marriage, marriage of highest promise, is again performed for time and for all eternity by qualified officiators in the holy temples of the Lord.

But a marriage designed to last forever will be a good marriage, growing and gracious. Sometimes the distinctive elements of temple marriage are thought of as being exclusive in duration and authority. Of course, everyone who comes to the temple to be married understands that the ceremony is performed by God's authority for time and eternity. But the remarkable revealed

Marion D. Hanks has served as a member of the First Quorum of the Seventy and as president of the British Mission. He and his wife, Maxine, served as president and matron of the Salt Lake Temple. They are the parents of five children.

ceremony at the altar in a temple contemplates *much more* than this. The quality of the relationship thus established is of highest importance. Wonderful promises are sealed upon a man and woman in temple marriage, and the realization of the promised blessings is related directly to their understanding and keeping the solemn commitments they make to each other and the Lord.

Those commitments in a temple are total and permanent—involving the whole person, *as is,* for the whole journey. Neither will remain as he or she is, of course; they will both grow and develop in a multitude of ways. But this marriage ceremony is without condition or reservation, save only the faithfulness of those who make it. On this solid foundation, the newly formed family joyfully undertakes to learn how to live happily forever, to build a strong and loving union that will grow more wholesome and more glorious everlastingly. How do we ensure success in such a vital and great undertaking?

Many new and enduring relationships spring into being with marriage—relationships all of which are vital to the happiness of the family.

For her, the words—sacred words—are *wife, mother, home-maker, heart* of the home; for him, *husband, father, protector, provider, leader* in the home in the warm spirit of the priesthood.

Together they enter a *partnership,* sharing and learning and growing.

They join their lives as *companions* in the special sense that married people do. Whether in the same room or a world apart, they are married twenty-four hours a day. They care about the whole person, the whole future of each other. With good humor and good disposition and genuine consideration of the needs of the other, they set out to *make* it a happy life. They laugh a lot and cry a little. They are warm and considerate and thoughtful: the note, the telephone call, the kind word, the sensitive response, the excitement of heading home to her, of having him come home.

Married people are *sweethearts,* in a special creative union, blessed with that powerful chemistry that draws two together, sometimes from next door, sometimes from a world away. This divinely designed power must be sustained by other qualities—by respect and loyalty and integrity—to be what it is meant to be. To be able to give oneself fully with confidence and trust, and to fully receive the other joyfully and gratefully—this is a blessing that grows in meaning year by year and forever.

And married people should be *best friends;* no relationship on earth needs friendship as much as marriage.

I have in my possession a letter written by a young widowed

immigrant in the early days of the Church. It was written in 1848 in Honeycreek, Missouri, to her husband's mother and sister in England. He had died on the sailing vessel en route, leaving her and the two boys to make their way west with the Saints, heart-sick and alone. She wrote a letter that changed my life a little. Maybe it will yours.

She began, "Dear Mother and dear Hannah, your dearly beloved son and my best friend has gone the way of all the earth. Dearer to me in life than life itself, he's gone. Oh Mother, Mother, what am I to do?"

And then she told of her love for this, her *best friend,* and that she would rear these two boys in the kingdom and in his image and in the admonition of the Lord.

A tear came as I asked myself if that letter could have been written at my house.

Friendship in a marriage is so important. It blows away the chaff and takes the kernel, rejoices in the uniqueness of the other, listens patiently, gives generously, forgives freely. Friendship will motivate one to cross the room one day and say, "I'm sorry; I didn't mean that." It will not pretend perfection nor demand it. It will not insist that both respond exactly the same in every thought and feeling, but it will bring to the union honesty, integrity. There will be repentance and forgiveness in every marriage—every good marriage—and respect and trust.

And all these and other elements we are not able to mention eloquently declare that such a union doesn't just *happen*.

So the need becomes clear for careful, thoughtful preparation, selection, and courtship. No one should be unwise enough to count on an across-the-crowded-room romanticized live-happily-ever-after marriage made without proper thoughtfulness, preparation, and prayer. Marriage is an everyday and every-way relationship in which honesty and character and shared convictions and objectives and views about finances and family and lifestyle are more important than moonlight and music and an attractive profile.

See Marion D. Hanks, "Eternal Marriage," Ensign, *November 1984, 35.*

"Do Well Those Things Which God Ordained"

Virginia U. Jensen

Each of us needs the steadying hands of loving family members on the trek back to our eternal home. It is in our earthly homes we have the greatest opportunities to reach out to one another, to provide that substantive, steadfast help that is necessary for an eternally successful completion to this life's journey.

President Joseph F. Smith reminded us that "to do well those things which God ordained to be the common lot of all man-kind, is the truest greatness. To be a successful father or a successful mother is greater than to be a successful general or a successful statesman" (*Gospel Doctrine* [Salt Lake City: Deseret Book, 1986], 150).

My life experience has taught me that all women striving for

Virginia U. Jensen has served as first counselor in the Relief Society general presidency. A homemaker who enjoys gardening, grandchildren, and family activities, she and her husband, J. Rees Jensen, are the parents of four children.

righteousness have a deep understanding of President Smith's statement.

Indeed, faithful women bring to all their relationships a profound respect for family and the roles they play in their own families. Our family responsibilities mean a great deal to us, whatever our circumstances. This is as the Lord would have it. After all, Eve was called "the mother of all living" long before she bore any children.

My hope is that all of us, sisters of Zion in many lands, will unite in a sacred recommitment to the holy calling of mothering and to "do[ing] well those things which God ordained." Each of us—single or married, having borne children or able to nurture and bless God's children whom we haven't given birth to—has much to offer.

Children, who are our literal legacy from the Lord, require our diligent, prayerful, loving mothering. And whether a woman has children in her home or not, each woman can exercise her gift of mothering in her extended family, in her Church callings, and in a variety of other settings. I would like to talk about three vital aspects of mothering: testimony, teaching, and time.

Testimony. President Heber J. Grant declared, "The mother in the family . . . is the one who instills in the hearts of the children, a testimony and a love for the gospel . . . ; and wherever you find a woman who is devoted to this work, almost without exception you will find that her children are devoted to it" (*Gospel Standards,* comp. G. Homer Durham [Salt Lake City: Deseret Book, 1941], 150).

Do your children and family members know you have a testimony? Does your knowledge of the restored gospel and the plan of salvation serve your children as they combat Satan's influence in a world of shifting values?

Testimony is an all-important element in family life. We view our family relationships as the building blocks of eternity. We build homes inside of houses. We love, nurture, and pray with and for each family member. Generation after generation of righteous children, youth, and adults comes from homes, mothers, and family members whose lives reflect their testimonies.

Teaching. The world offers far too many substitute teachers to show our children alternate paths if we do not endeavor to teach them how to walk "the straight way." Any woman who doubts the significance or centrality of her place in the Church should realize that prophets learn their first gospel lessons from mothers in their homes. It is in the home that our children learn about the Savior and the important gospel truths that will lead them back to their heavenly home. It is the mother who most consistently encourages her sons to advance in the priesthood and to prepare to serve missions; it is the mother who teaches her daughters to dress modestly and live worthily to enter the temple. Every mother is a teacher. No formal degree is required, but your determination to instruct prayerfully and lovingly and according to God's plan is prerequisite to your success—and theirs. We must teach our children the things of God, the mission of Christ, and their plan for eternal happiness. Just as we strive to sustain our children temporally, we must teach them the lessons of eternity, or we will deprive them of what they really need to survive spiritually.

Time. Our total focus of time, energy, spirit, and heart on our God-ordained role brings the greatest rewards for ourselves and our family members. We can become confused by things that seem important and spend our time and energy in the name of many good things while neglecting that which is of highest value—our families. It is easy to become distracted with so many things competing for our time. The prize is so great that Satan wants us to get sidetracked. Eternity lies before us, but mortal life is the period in which children of God learn the lessons that enable eternal progression. How we choose to spend each moment of life determines the degree of success we'll have in teaching our families and strengthening their testimonies.

Women have many choices and many obligations, but the truth remains that the most important thing we can do with our time is to strengthen our family members.

The Savior taught us about priorities when he said, "Lay not up for yourselves treasures on earth, . . . but lay up for yourselves treasures in heaven, . . . for where your treasure is, there will your heart be also" (3 Nephi 13:19–21).

Make home and family your treasure. Wholeheartedly give them your time, energy, and avid attention.

Only you can determine the most important use of your time. But remember the routine, small acts that take place in the home are the building blocks of eternal relationships. In the informal discussions at the dinner table or while working at daily tasks come the moments to teach and observe. In the day in and day out of family life, children can come to know and love Heavenly Father and our Savior, Jesus Christ, in ways no Church activity can ever duplicate or teach.

President Joseph F. Smith taught us a potent truth when he counseled us "to do well those things which God ordained to be the common lot of all man-kind." The daily business of motherhood often seems common indeed, but you, the women of Zion, are uncommonly good.

See Virginia U. Jensen, "'Do Well Those Things Which God Ordained,'" Ye Shall Bear Record of Me (Salt Lake City: Deseret Book, 2002), 197.

A Prelude to Heaven

Albert Choules Jr.

When asked to define "the first commandment of all," the Savior answered, "Thou shalt love the Lord thy God with all thy heart, and with all thy soul, and with all thy mind, and with all thy strength" (Mark 12:28, 30). Therefore, obedience to this commandment should become our highest priority. All of our efforts should evidence love for our Father in Heaven.

Jesus indicated several ways to demonstrate the love we should have for him and for our Heavenly Father but phrased it concisely in the simple statement, "If ye love me, keep my commandments" (John 14:15).

Then our Savior added another short and easily understood statement: "Love one another" (John 13:34). Our love of God

---

Albert Choules Jr., formerly president of a large hotel chain, has served as a member of both the First and the Second Quorums of the Seventy. He and his late wife, Rosemary, became the parents of three children. He married Marilyn Jeppson Lowry in 1987.

and Jesus Christ and for each other should undergird all that we do and feel. Love sincerely given brings love in return. Love so shared brings trust, support, and a level of security that is unsurpassed. A child naturally nestles in the arms of his or her mother, seeking love and protection from her who gave life. That kind of innate love seems to exemplify the commandment to love one another. Love of others seems to come so naturally to children. Their expectation of love in return seems also to be inborn.

These typical tendencies for children to love became especially apparent to me on my first visit to Romania. I remember it vividly. Sister Choules and I went to various institutions with our humanitarian missionaries who were serving there. At an orphanage we saw a rather long, narrow, glass-enclosed room where twenty or so children were playing. They were about three years of age. Most of their daytime hours were spent entertaining themselves and each other, apparently with very little adult care. I asked the supervisor if I could open the door and take some pictures. She agreed. Upon opening the door, many of the children rushed out. I was reminded of days in my youth, when in like manner I saw cattle and horses rush to freedom when a corral gate was opened. These children, however, were not rushing to be free. They hungered for love. Soon we had one or more grasping at each of our legs, reaching up for the love for which they were so starved. I'll forever have in my mind the picture I took of Sister Choules holding one of these children with their arms tightly wrapped around each other. These children just wanted to be loved and to give love in return. These little ones and other children seem to be born with that unrestrained desire and capacity.

But as we get older, something seems to get in the way. It seems more difficult to give and receive sincere love as children do so naturally. The Lord not only said "Love one another" but he prefaced those words with "A new commandment I give unto you, That ye love one another." Then he taught the kind of love that we should cultivate when he added, "As I have loved you, that ye also love one another" (John 13:34).

Often I have wondered: Why do we as adults have to be commanded to do that which comes so naturally to children? Perhaps that is why Christ said that each of us should strive to become as a little child, "for of such is the kingdom of heaven" (Matthew 19:14).

The kingdom of heaven for which we strive can begin with a heavenly life here and now. We can develop a child's love matured. President David O. McKay said:

"I know of no other place than home where more happiness can be found in this life. It is possible to make home a bit of heaven; indeed, I picture heaven to be a continuation of the ideal home. Some man has said: 'Home filled with contentment is one of the highest hopes of this life'" (Conference Report, April 1964, 5; or *Improvement Era*, June 1964, 520).

How do we make our home the ideal home and the proper prelude to heaven? I believe we start with the Savior's admonition to keep his commandments and to do so specifically within the walls of our own home. Husband and wife—father and mother—set the example and tone for all that happens within the home. Hopefully, the relationship starts at a sacred altar in a holy temple. There they kneel, knowing that they are both worthy of that sacred privilege. They are prepared and desirous of entering into sacred covenants—to put each other and the goal of being together in heaven first in their lives. Selfishness is to be put aside. They begin a partnership—a full partnership—that is to be eternal. When true love prevails between husband and wife, they want to give themselves to and for each other, as Christ gave of himself. We give for each other on a daily basis when we endeavor always to make each other happy. Then we give up thinking selfishly of ourselves and our personal needs. Then we really think not only of the here and now but of the hereafter.

The Savior has told us that if we marry "by my word, which is my law, and by the new and everlasting covenant, . . . and if ye abide in my covenant, . . . it shall be done unto them in all things whatsoever my servant hath put upon them, in time, and through all eternity; and shall be of full force when they are out of the world; and they shall pass by the angels, and the gods, which are set there, to their exaltation and glory in all things, as hath been sealed upon their heads, which glory shall be a fulness and a continuation of the seeds forever and ever" (D&C 132:19). These are the great and marvelous blessings of exaltation, glory, and eternal life. They are only sealed upon us in the holy temples. They can indeed be ours. With that eternal perspective, only loving thoughts and actions should prevail in our homes, where we help each other along the road to exaltation. That perspective not only prepares us for eternity, but it makes the here and now much happier and more fulfilling.

———

See Albert Choules Jr., "A Child's Love Matured," Ensign, May 1994, 13.

Righteous Unity

~

Ezra Taft Benson

Marriage is the rock foundation, the cornerstone, of civilization. No nation will ever rise above its homes.

Marriage and family life are ordained of God.

In an eternal sense, salvation is a family affair. God holds parents responsible for their stewardship in rearing their family. It is a most sacred responsibility.

My message is to return to the God-ordained fundamentals that will ensure love, stability, and happiness in our homes. One fundamental to happy, enduring family relationships is:

A husband and wife must attain righteous unity and oneness in their goals, desires, and actions.

Marriage itself must be regarded as a sacred covenant before

Ezra Taft Benson, who served as secretary of agriculture under U.S. president Dwight D. Eisenhower, was ordained an apostle in 1943 and sustained as president of the Church in 1985. He and his wife, Flora Amussen Benson, became the parents of six children. President Benson died in 1994 at the age of ninety-four.

God. A married couple have an obligation not only to each other, but to God. He has promised blessings to those who honor that covenant.

Fidelity to one's marriage vows is absolutely essential for love, trust, and peace. Adultery is unequivocally condemned by the Lord.

Husbands and wives who love each other will find that love and loyalty are reciprocated. This love will provide a nurturing atmosphere for the emotional growth of children. Family life should be a time of happiness and joy that children can look back on with fond memories and associations.

Hear these simple admonitions from the Lord which may be applied to the marriage covenant.

First: "See that ye love one another; cease to be covetous; learn to impart one to another as the gospel requires. . . . Cease to be unclean; cease to find fault one with another" (D&C 88:123–24).

Second: "Thou shalt love thy wife with all thy heart, and shalt cleave unto her and none else. . . . Thou shalt not commit adultery" (D&C 42:22, 24).

Third: "He that hath the spirit of contention is not of me, but is of the devil, who is the father of contention" (3 Nephi 11:29).

And there are many more scriptural admonitions.

Restraint and self-control must be ruling principles in the marriage relationship. Couples must learn to bridle their tongues as well as their passions.

Prayer in the home and prayer with each other will strengthen your union. Gradually, thoughts, aspirations, and ideas will merge into a oneness until you are seeking the same purposes and goals.

Rely on the Lord, the teachings of the prophets, and the scriptures for guidance and help, particularly when there may be disagreements and problems.

Spiritual growth comes by solving problems together—not by running from them. Today's inordinate emphasis on individualism brings egotism and separation. Two individuals becoming "one flesh" is still the Lord's standard (Genesis 2:24).

The secret of a happy marriage is to serve God and each other. The goal of marriage is unity and oneness, as well as self-development. Paradoxically, the more we serve one another, the greater is our spiritual and emotional growth.

———

See Ezra Taft Benson, "Fundamentals of Enduring Family Relationships," Ensign, *November 1982, 59.*

Part Six

We Find Nobility
in Motherhood and
Joy in Womanhood

THE JOY OF WOMANHOOD

Margaret D. Nadauld

That women were born into this earth female was determined long before mortal birth, as were the divine differences of male and female. I love the clarity of the teachings of the First Presidency and the Quorum of the Twelve in the proclamation on the family, in which they state, "Gender is an essential characteristic of individual premortal, mortal, and eternal identity and purpose" ("The Family: A Proclamation to the World," *Ensign*, November 1995, 102). From that statement we are taught that every girl was feminine and female in spirit long before her mortal birth.

God sent women to earth with some qualities in extra capacity. In speaking to young women, President James E. Faust observed

---

Margaret D. Nadauld has served as a member of the Relief Society general board and as Young Women general president. She and her husband, Stephen D. Nadauld, a former member of the Second Quorum of the Seventy, are the parents of seven children.

that femininity "is the divine adornment of humanity. It finds expression in your . . . capacity to love, your spirituality, delicacy, radiance, sensitivity, creativity, charm, graciousness, gentleness, dignity, and quiet strength. It is manifest differently in each girl or woman, but each . . . possesses it. Femininity is part of your inner beauty" ("Womanhood, the Highest Place of Honor," *Ensign,* May 2000, 96).

Our outward appearance is a reflection of what we are on the inside. Our lives reflect that for which we seek. And if with all our hearts we truly seek to know the Savior and to be more like him, we shall be, for he is our divine, eternal Brother.

You can recognize women who are grateful to be a daughter of God by their outward appearance. These women understand their stewardship over their bodies and treat them with dignity. They care for their bodies as they would a holy temple, for they understand the Lord's teaching: "Know ye not that ye are the temple of God, and that the Spirit of God dwelleth in you?" (1 Corinthians 3:16). Women who love God would never abuse or deface a temple with graffiti. Nor would they throw open the doors of that holy, dedicated edifice and invite the world to look on. How even more sacred is the body, for it was not made by man. It was formed by God. We are the stewards, the keepers of the cleanliness and purity with which it came from heaven. "If any man defile the temple of

God, him shall God destroy; for the temple of God is holy, which temple ye are" (1 Corinthians 3:17).

Grateful daughters of God guard their bodies carefully, for they know they are the wellspring of life and they reverence life. They don't uncover their bodies to find favor with the world. They walk in modesty to be in favor with their Father in Heaven, for they know he loves them dearly.

You can recognize women who are grateful to be a daughter of God by their attitude. They know that the errand of angels is given to women, and they desire to be on God's errand to love his children and minister to them, to teach them the doctrines of salvation, to call them to repentance, to save them in perilous circumstances, to guide them in the performance of his work, to deliver his messages (Bruce R. McConkie, *Mormon Doctrine,* 2d ed. [Salt Lake City: Bookcraft, 1966], 35). They understand that they can bless their Father's children in their homes and neighborhoods and beyond. Women who are grateful to be daughters of God bring glory to his name.

You can recognize women who are grateful to be a daughter of God by their abilities. They fulfill their divine potential and magnify their God-given gifts. They are capable, strong women who bless families, serve others, and understand that "the glory of God is intelligence" (D&C 93:36). They are women who embrace enduring virtues in order to be all that our Father needs them to be. The prophet Jacob spoke of some of those virtues when he said their "feelings are exceedingly tender and chaste and delicate before God, which thing is pleasing unto God" (Jacob 2:7).

You can recognize women who are grateful to be a daughter of God by their reverence for motherhood, even when that blessing has been withheld from them for a time. In those circumstances, their righteous influence can be a blessing in the lives of children they love. Their exemplary teachings can echo the voice of a faithful home and resonate truth in the hearts of children who need another witness.

Grateful daughters of God love him and teach their children to love him without reservation and without resentment. They are like the mothers of Helaman's youthful army, who had such great faith and "had been taught by their mothers, that if they did not doubt, God would deliver them" (Alma 56:47).

They understand what Elder Neal A. Maxwell meant when he said: "When the real history of mankind is fully disclosed, will it feature the echoes of gunfire or the shaping sound of lullabies? The great armistices made by military men or the peacemaking of women in homes and in neighborhoods? Will what happened in cradles and kitchens prove to be more controlling than what happened in congresses?" ("The Women of God," *Ensign*, May 1978, 10–11).

Daughters of God know that it is the nurturing nature of women that can bring everlasting blessings, and they live to cultivate this divine attribute. Surely when a woman reverences motherhood, her children will arise up and call her blessed (Proverbs 31:28).

Women of God can never be like women of the world. The world has enough women who are tough; we need women who are tender. There are enough women who are coarse; we need women who are kind. There are enough women who are rude; we need women who are refined. We have enough women of fame and fortune; we need more women of faith. We have enough greed; we need more goodness. We have enough vanity; we need more virtue. We have enough popularity; we need more purity.

We must understand all that we are and must be, all that we were prepared to be in royal courts on high by God himself. May we use with gratitude the priceless gifts we have been given for the lifting of mankind to higher thinking and nobler aspirations.

———

See Margaret D. Nadauld, "The Joy of Womanhood," Ensign, *November 2000, 14.*

CELEBRATING WOMANHOOD

Marie K. Hafen

My voice of celebration is a voice of hope, yet also a voice of warning, because the confusion in modern society can confuse all of us about the aspirations of women. Remember the Savior's words: "Behold, I send you forth as sheep in the midst of wolves: be ye therefore wise as serpents, and harmless as doves" (Matthew 10:16). Wisdom and meekness help us keep our balance in these unstable times.

Soon after my husband, Bruce, and I were blessed with children, we discovered that, as someone said, "To believe in God is to know that the eternal rules are fair, and that there will be some wonderful surprises." One of those wonderful surprises was to

---

Marie Kartchner Hafen has served on the Young Women general board and on the board of the Deseret News. She has taught writing and Shakespeare courses at Brigham Young University and BYU–Idaho. She and her husband, Bruce C. Hafen, a member of the First Quorum of the Seventy, are the parents of seven children.

learn what Lehi meant when he said that if Adam and Eve had remained in the Garden of Eden, "they would have had no children; . . . they would have remained in a state of innocence, having no joy, for they knew no misery" (2 Nephi 2:23). Astute parents will note here that if Adam and Eve had had no *children,* they would have had no *misery!* But note also that without children and misery, they would have had no *joy.* And two verses further, Lehi tells us that "men are, that they might have joy" (2 Nephi 2:25).

Now that I've had a house full of children and grandchildren and their not-always-wonderful surprises for more than thirty years, *all* of Lehi's words have meaning for me. Of course, there are days of drudgery. Dishes get dirty, children cry, and family members get sick. There are bills to pay and cars to fix, too little time and not enough money. There is frustration and fatigue and disappointment. Yet somehow, amid this sometimes drab reality, there are moments of genuine joy and meaning so tender that all you can do is kneel to thank God through your tears for the gift of children and the bonds of married love.

King Benjamin spoke of the "happy state of those that keep the commandments of God" and are "blessed in all things, both temporal and spiritual" (Mosiah 2:41). Does this mean that if people keep the basic commandments, they won't have any problems?

Lehi taught us that if Adam and Eve had remained in Eden, they would have remained not in a state of true happiness, but "in a state of *innocence*"—having no children, no misery, no sin—*and no joy* (2 Nephi 2:23; italics added). So when King Benjamin tells us of the "blessed and happy state" of those who keep God's commandments, he is not describing a Kingdom of Oz where there are no witches. On the contrary, developing the strength that leads to authentic joy requires us to follow the Adamic pattern into a world of thorns and sorrow.

Adam and Eve fell that they might have joy. But they didn't skip merrily out of Eden singing and wishing everyone a nice day. They walked in sorrow into a lonely world, where they earned their bread by the sweat of their brows and learned about joy in the midst of misery and pain. Can you imagine how Eve felt when she learned that her son Cain had taken the life of her son Abel and that God had banished Cain?

How could Mother Eve possibly have found joy in the middle of such affliction? She found it by letting the atonement of Christ heal her pain and sanctify her experience. Indeed, her experience with sin and misery played a crucial role in preparing her for the joy she ultimately found. In Eve's own words, "Were it not for our transgression we never should have had seed, and never should have known good and evil, and the joy of our redemption, and the eternal life which God giveth unto all the obedient" (Moses 5:11).

Women in the modern world, like women in the ancient world, go forth as sheep in the midst of wolves. In such a world, we must be spiritually strong and wise, like Mother Eve, who "ceased not to call upon God" (Moses 5:16).

Women who are prepared for life can celebrate with confidence. Never have opportunities for prepared women been greater—in the home, in the Church, and in the community.

I rejoice in the seasons of a woman's life, for each time and each season is worth its own celebration. Spread over a lifetime, celebrating womanhood is a celebration of life.

———

See Marie K. Hafen, "Celebrating Womanhood," Ensign, June 1992, 50.

Leading, Loving, Listening

Sharon G. Larsen

Love is listening when *they* are ready to talk—midnight, 6 A.M. on their way to seminary, or when you're busy with your urgencies. Have you seen the Church spot on television showing a darkened bedroom? The door opens, and in walks a little girl with a book under her arm. She goes over to where her dad is sound asleep and asks, "Daddy, will you read me a story?" The dad doesn't open his eyes; he just mumbles in his sleep, "Oh, honey, Daddy is so tired. Ask Mommy." The little girl patters over to where her mother is sleeping and asks, "Mommy, can Daddy read me a story?" You see the dad's eyes pop open, and the next picture shows all three of them together, and Dad is reading a story.

Loving may come naturally, but leading is a polished skill that

---

Sharon G. Larsen has served on the Young Women general board and as second counselor in the Young Women general presidency. A writer and schoolteacher, she has also taught seminary and institute. She and her husband, Ralph T. Larsen, are the parents of two children.

maybe we don't take seriously enough. We lead by example more strongly than any other way. That is a heavy burden for parents and leaders of youth.

Can our young people tell by the way we live and talk and pray that we love the Lord? Do they know that their Father in Heaven is a God of love by the way they feel when they are with us? Can they feel secure that we will not be moved by every wind of doctrine or the craftiness of social pressure and worldly acceptance? (Ephesians 4:14).

If we are going to lead in righteousness, there can't be any question where we stand. Small uncertainties on our part can produce large uncertainties in our youth.

I wonder sometimes if we as mothers are the ones who make our children feel the pressure to be popular and accepted. Educating our desires so our standards are the Lord's standards sends a clear message that in the Lord's kingdom there are no double standards.

Following President Gordon B. Hinckley's talk to the youth some time ago, a young woman reported to her mother that her Young Women leader had removed her second set of earrings. These scrutinizing young people notice. They notice how short your shorts are or if you had to tuck and pin to wear that blouse; they notice what you wear (or don't wear) when you are working in your yard; they notice which line you are standing in at the movie theater.

We have made covenants with the Lord, and leading often tests the level of our commitment to those covenants.

A young mother said, "It takes an enormous amount of time and energy to be a good parent. It is easier to let my children fall asleep in front of the television while I pick up the house and then put them to bed than it is to read the scriptures to them, have prayers and stories, and tuck them in. But they look forward to this evening ritual, and I know this investment, even when I'm too tired to move, will pay eternal dividends." Consistent leading helps youth make wise choices, and our trust in them increases.

I remember when I was about sixteen years old overhearing Mom talking to Dad. She was concerned about some choices I was making. I was not guilty of any sin more serious than the immaturity of youth, but Mom was worried. What Dad said seared into my heart. "Don't worry," he said to Mom. "I trust Sharon, and I know she'll do the right thing." The hours we had spent working together in the hayfield paid off then and there. From that moment on, I was bound to those loving, trusting parents.

One of the greatest tests for parents and leaders is to love the one who seems to be unlovable. This is tough duty. It stretches the heartstrings and wrenches the soul. When heartbroken parents pray for help, the help often comes in the form of angel aunts or uncles, grandmas or grandpas, good friends, and leaders surrounding our loved one. They can reinforce our very message that may put our child on the track we've been praying for.

Loving wisely and leading purposefully will help stem the tide of wickedness as we prepare the next generation for the exhilarating delights of parenthood. We never forget the joys of our twelve-year-old when he first passes the sacrament or hearing the sacramental prayer given in the voice of our son. How do you explain the feeling of hearing your daughter bear her testimony of the Savior or watching her receive her Young Womanhood medallion?

We catch a glimpse of heaven when we are in the temple with our child who is kneeling across the altar from a worthy companion. They are prepared to start a life together of promise and accomplishments that we have helped to nurture. This is harvest time.

I testify that we are not alone in this sacred trust of parenting, loving, and leading. There is no greater joy. It is worth every sacrifice, every inconvenient minute, every ounce of patience, personal discipline, and endurance. "If God be for us, who can be against us?" (Romans 8:31).

See Sharon G. Larsen, "Fear Not: For They That Be with Us Are More," Ensign, *November 2001, 67.*

A Godly Responsibility

Patricia P. Pinegar

Parenting is a godly responsibility necessary for the salvation of Father's children and important for our preparation for eternal blessings. Rejoice in your opportunities to love and care for the souls of children. Our Father has blessings and eternal rewards available for each of his children, whether they are married or single, parents or childless. Our circumstances may be different, our opportunities may be varied, but the end result of our righteousness can be the same—eternal parenthood, eternal lives. Helping to care for the souls of children will help each of us prepare for this eternal blessing.

What are some things that we can do to improve? I believe that seriously studying how our Father cares for his children can

Patricia P. Pinegar has served as Primary general president. She and her husband, Ed J. Pinegar, have filled missions together in England and at the Missionary Training Center in Provo, Utah. They are the parents of eight children.

help us. Everything we know about our Heavenly Father is connected with his parenthood and his loving care for our souls. He loves each of his children unconditionally. We can do the same in our families. His plan of happiness is a plan to help his children progress and be prepared to receive his greatest blessings. We can make plans to help our families progress. He included his children in the great Heavenly Council and allowed us to participate and use our agency to choose. We can have family councils and include our children as active participants. Under his guidance, this earth was prepared as a place where we could learn and grow. Our homes can be happy places where our children can learn and grow. He has given his children rules of conduct and commandments that keep us moving forward, focused on the path that leads to our heavenly home. The rules of conduct in our family can help us move forward on the path back to our Heavenly Father.

The Only Begotten Son of our Father, our Savior Jesus Christ, spent his earthly ministry showing us how to love, bless, and teach all of the family of God. He taught us that not one soul should be lost. We should follow his example in loving and blessing our families and doing all we can to see that not one soul is lost.

Work toward being temple worthy, and obtain a temple recommend even if the temple is too far away to attend very often. Great blessings will come to you and your children because of your personal righteousness. If you now have a temple recommend, study and pray and attend the temple often to increase your understanding of the covenants you have made.

Each parent also needs to follow this counsel from President Hinckley: "You need more than your own wisdom in rearing [your children]. You need the help of the Lord. Pray for that help and follow the inspiration which you receive" ("The Fabric and Faith of Testimony," *Ensign,* November 1995, 89).

As we become more righteous by keeping our covenants and by more closely following the counsel in the scriptures and from our living prophets, we will truly be blessed with the daily guidance that we need from our Father and Savior to raise our children in righteousness.

To all fathers and mothers of the Church, tell your children that you love them and that you are so happy to have them in your family. Prepare yourselves spiritually to receive the guidance through the Holy Ghost. As you prayerfully study the scriptures and "The Family: A Proclamation to the World" (*Ensign,* November 1995, 102), listen and respond to the promptings of the Spirit. Be aware of Satan's influences. Where do the feelings come from that make you feel that your efforts in the home are not fulfilling or important? Where do the feelings come from that make you feel unappreciated? Rejoice in this preparation for godhood. Rejoice in the opportunity to teach your children the truths of the kingdom, and help them experience the peace and joy that comes from following these truths.

———

See Patricia P. Pinegar, "Caring for the Souls of Children," Ensign, May *1997, 13.*

You Are Chosen

Howard W. Hunter

As our Lord and Savior needed the women of his time for a comforting hand, a listening ear, a believing heart, a kind look, an encouraging word, loyalty—even in his hour of humiliation, agony, and death—so we, his servants all across the Church, need you, the women of the Church, to stand with us and for us in stemming the tide of evil that threatens to engulf us. Together we must stand faithful and firm in the faith against superior numbers of other-minded people. It seems to me that there is a great need to rally the women of the Church to stand with and for the Brethren in stemming the tide of evil that surrounds us and in moving forward the work of our Savior. Nephi said, "Ye must

---

Howard W. Hunter was ordained an apostle by David O. McKay in 1959 and sustained president of the Church in 1994. He and Claire Jeffs were married in the Salt Lake Temple in 1931 and became the parents of three children. After her death, he married Inis Bernice Egan. President Hunter died in 1995 at the age of eighty-seven.

press forward with a steadfastness in Christ, having a perfect brightness of hope, and a love of God and of all men, [women, and children]" (2 Nephi 31:20). Obedient to him, we are a majority. But only together can we accomplish the work he has given us to do and be prepared for the day when we shall see him.

Those who follow Christ seek to follow his example. His suffering on behalf of our sins, shortcomings, sorrows, and sicknesses should motivate us to similarly reach out in charity and compassion to those around us. It is most appropriate that the motto of the longest-standing women's organization in the world—the Relief Society of The Church of Jesus Christ of Latter-day Saints—is Charity Never Faileth.

Sisters, continue to seek opportunities for service. Don't be overly concerned with status. Do you recall the counsel of the Savior regarding those who seek the "chief seats" or the "uppermost rooms"? "He that is greatest among you shall be your servant" (Matthew 23:6, 11). It is important to be appreciated. But our focus should be on righteousness, not recognition; on service, not status. The faithful visiting teacher, who quietly goes about her work month after month, is just as important to the work of the Lord as those who occupy what some see as more prominent positions in the Church. Visibility does not equate to value.

In a general meeting of the women of the Church, President Spencer W. Kimball counseled: "Bear in mind, dear sisters, that the eternal blessings which are yours through membership in The Church of Jesus Christ of Latter-day Saints are far, far greater than any other blessings you could possibly receive. No greater recognition can come to you in this world than to be known as a woman of God. No greater status can be conferred upon you than being a daughter of God who experiences true sisterhood, wifehood, and motherhood, or other tasks which influence lives for good" ("The Role of Righteous Women," *Ensign,* November 1979, 102).

You are chosen to be faithful women of God in our day, to stand above pettiness, gossip, selfishness, lewdness, and all other forms of ungodliness.

Recognize your divine birthright as daughters of our Heavenly Father. Be one who heals with your words as well as your hands. Seek to know the will of the Lord in your life, and then say, as did that wonderful exemplar Mary, the mother of Jesus, "Behold the handmaid of the Lord; be it unto me according to thy word" (Luke 1:38).

In conclusion, these verses from an unknown poet have significant meaning:

They talk about a woman's sphere,
As though it has a limit;
There's not a place in earth or heaven,
There's not a task to mankind given,
There's not a blessing nor a woe,
There's not a whispered yes or no,
There's not a life, or death, or birth,
That has a feather's weight of worth . . .
Without a woman in it.

———

See Howard W. Hunter, "To the Women of the Church," Ensign, November 1992, 95.

Part Seven

We Delight
in Service and
Good Works

ARISE, SHINE FORTH, AND SERVE

Mary Ellen Smoot

During some of the darkest days of the Church, when the Saints were facing terrible persecution in Far West, Missouri, the Prophet Joseph Smith revealed the will of the Lord for the Saints then and for you and me now: "Arise and shine forth, that thy light may be a standard for the nations" (D&C 115:5).

This admonition still applies today. At a general Relief Society meeting, President Gordon B. Hinckley, our prophet, gave us the charge: "If anyone can change the dismal situation into which we are sliding, it is you. Rise up, O women of Zion, rise to the great challenge which faces you" ("Walking in the Light of the Lord," *Ensign,* November 1998, 99).

Mary Ellen Smoot, who loves family history and has written several histories of parents, grandparents, and their local community, has served as general president of the Relief Society. She served with her husband, Stanley M. Smoot, when he was called as mission president in Ohio. They are the parents of seven children.

If we are to be a "standard for the nations," we must arise in loving service. The Relief Society Declaration reminds us that as Relief Society sisters we "delight in service and good works" ("Relief Society Declaration," *Ensign,* November 1999, 93). If we are to rise up and really serve others, we must understand and embrace the mission of Relief Society. Relief Society sisters are an integral part of our spiritual safety.

When the first twenty Relief Society sisters gathered in Nauvoo and were deciding on a name for their organization, Eliza R. Snow suggested the word *relief* because it implied service both common and extraordinary. Emma Smith, the newly set-apart president, liked the idea and said, "We expect extraordinary occasions and pressing calls" ("A Record of the Organization, and Proceedings of the Female Relief Society of Nauvoo," 17 March 1842, Archives of The Church of Jesus Christ of Latter-day Saints, Salt Lake City). The Prophet Joseph Smith had been asked to be in attendance, and he stated, "With the resources [the Relief Society sisters] will have at their command, they will fly to the relief of the stranger; they will pour in oil . . . to the wounded heart of the distressed; they will dry up the tears of the orphan and make the widow's heart to rejoice" (*History of The Church of Jesus Christ of Latter-day Saints,* ed. B. H. Roberts, 2d ed. rev., 7 vols. [Salt Lake City: Deseret Book, 1932–51], 4:567).

As the tide of selfishness sends its waves so high in the world, we can determine to change that tide by being pure vessels of Christlike love and service. Service is the essence of Christ's gospel. Service is the antidote to the ills of our time. Service heals the wounded heart. President Hinckley made this observation: "Generally speaking, the most miserable people I know are those who are obsessed with themselves, the happiest people I know are those who lose themselves in the service of others. . . . The most effective medicine for the sickness of self-pity is to lose ourselves in the service of others" (*Teachings of Gordon B. Hinckley* [Salt Lake City: Deseret Book, 1997], 589–90).

No matter what your circumstances, "charity never faileth." This Relief Society motto and the new Relief Society Declaration are not just samplers that we hang on our walls; they must be inscribed in our hearts and become a way of life for us. Everything we do can be performed in a spirit of selfless love and service. Whether we are cleaning the house, shopping for groceries, talking with a friend, or visiting and teaching, we can be charitable.

The circumstances of each of us are unique, and each of us has her own gifts to give. You do what you can do. Don't "run faster than [you have] strength" (Mosiah 4:27). The Spirit will guide you in your efforts, and you will remember that "all these things are done in wisdom and order" (Mosiah 4:27). Relief

Society sisters all around the world are serving in so many different ways.

Loving service takes on so many different forms. Some of the most important services we ever perform are sharing the gospel of Jesus Christ and otherwise relieving spiritual suffering. The "casseroles" of faith and hope that we give to a friend, the "cookies" of kindness that we extend to our own families, the "coats" of charity that we gently place on others' shoulders when their hearts need spiritual warming—these are some of the most vital services. And many are performed within the walls of our own homes.

See Mary Ellen Smoot, "'Arise and Shine Forth,'" Arise and Shine Forth *(Salt Lake City: Deseret Book, 2001), 1.*

Love Extends
Beyond Convenience

J. Richard Clarke

In 1897 Dr. Charles Sheldon, a young minister in Topeka, Kansas, wrote a book which he titled *In His Steps*. It was a novel based upon an experiment he tried. He disguised himself as an unemployed printer and tramped the streets of Topeka. He was shocked at his treatment by this "Christian" community. In his novel, a Christian minister presents his congregation with this interesting challenge:

"I want volunteers . . . who will pledge themselves, earnestly and honestly for an entire year, not to do anything without first asking the question, 'What would Jesus do?' . . . Our aim will be to act just as He would if He [were] in our places, regardless of immediate results. In other words, we propose to follow Jesus' steps as

J. Richard Clarke has served as second counselor in the Presiding Bishopric and as a member of the First Quorum of the Seventy. He and his wife, Barbara Reed Clarke, are the parents of eight children.

closely and as literally as we believe He taught His disciples to do" (*In His Steps* [New York: Grosset & Dunlap, 1935], 15–16).

The book describes the fascinating experience of those who accepted the challenge. I have been intrigued by the experiment and wonder, if it were conducted today among the Latter-day Saints, how we would measure up. As latter-day Christians, we know that the "royal law" (James 2:8) of love in action is to "succor the weak, lift up the hands which hang down, and strengthen the feeble knees" (D&C 81:5). Do we catch the significance of this thought? We demonstrate the depth of our love for the Savior when we care enough to seek out the suffering among us and attend to their needs.

The philosopher William George Jordan has identified "four great hungers of life—body-hunger, mind-hunger, heart-hunger, and soul-hunger. They are all real; all need recognition, all need feeding" (*The Crown of Individuality* [New York: Fleming H. Revell Co., 1909], 63–75).

1. Body-hunger is our most conscious biological need. It is difficult to be spiritually strong when temporally deficient.

2. Mind-hunger is a craving for intellectual food, for education, and for personal development.

3. Heart-hunger is to be lonely, to have low self-esteem, to be misunderstood, to crave companionship, sympathy, and

appreciation. Paradoxically, we find that as we seek to satisfy the heart-hunger of our neighbor, we reduce our own.

4. Soul-hunger is the burning desire to know eternal truth. It is the yearning of the spirit to commune with God.

The restored gospel of Jesus Christ provides the solution to all the hungers of life. Jesus said: "I am the bread of life: he that cometh to me shall never hunger; and he that believeth on me shall never thirst" (John 6:35). We would all like to have the Savior's capacity to assuage the hungers of the world; but let us not forget that there are many simple ways by which we can walk in his steps. Let us remember that in giving of ourselves, it is less a question of giving a lot than of giving at the right moment.

How many times have we observed a benevolent act performed by someone and asked ourselves, "Why didn't I think of that?" Those who do the deeds we would have liked to do seem to have mastered the art of awareness. They have formed the habit of being sensitive to the needs of others before they think of themselves. How swiftly opportunity slips away, and we are left with another unfulfilled good intention. If only our acts of kindness could equal the righteous desires of our hearts.

Perhaps the most heroic acts are done quietly and with no recognition except from a loving Heavenly Father who rewards us with the sweet peace that passeth understanding (Philippians 4:7) and by his Spirit whispers, "Well done, [my] good and faithful servant" (Matthew 25:21).

I was touched by an experience someone related to me. A dear sister had been incapacitated for eight years—she could not walk or talk and was confined to bed. She and her husband were assigned a faithful home teacher, who asked if his wife could go over to their house every Sunday morning and stay with the invalid woman while her husband attended priesthood meeting. For six years, every Sunday this home teacher would take his wife to stay with the invalid sister while her husband went to his meeting. And every Sunday the home teacher's wife would take with her some baked goods or something special that she had made for this older couple.

Finally, the sister who had been ill passed away. When her daughter tried to express her deep love and appreciation to this loving home teacher and his wife for what they had done over the years, the wife said, "Oh, don't thank us. It was our *privilege* to visit with your sweet mother. What am I going to do now? The hour and a half on Sunday morning will now be, for me, the loneliest hour and a half in the week."

If we are to walk in the steps of the Savior, we cannot do it without personal sacrifice and sincere involvement. It is rarely convenient; but love extends beyond convenience for those who have conditioned themselves to look for opportunities to serve. I believe that the Savior was equipped to accomplish his mission not only through his parentage but because of his thirty years of preparation in developing an awareness of and a sensitivity to the needs of his fellowmen.

―――――

See J. Richard Clarke, "Love Extends beyond Convenience," Ensign, November 1981, 79.

The Power of Goodness

Janette Hales Beckham

The powers of heaven are available to everyone through righteousness. Mormon teaches that "every thing which inviteth to do good, and to persuade to believe in Christ, is sent forth by the *power* and gift of Christ" (Moroni 7:16; italics added).

A faithful member shared her testimony of how the *power* of goodness influenced her life. She writes:

"Until I was about eight years old, I was oblivious to the fact that my mother had serious health problems—later diagnosed as multiple sclerosis. When I was a first-year Beehive, I awoke one May morning to find that my mother was paralyzed from the neck down. She was already blind."

Confined to her bed, this courageous woman became the hub of the household. Her daughter wrote:

Janette Hales Beckham has served as general president of Young Women. She and her late husband, Robert H. Hales, became the parents of five children. She married Raymond E. Beckham in 1995.

"One day it fell upon me to clean the oven, a chore I approached with self-pity and much complaining. I went into her bedroom to whine a little and realized that Mom was crying. She said, 'Do you know how much I would give to be able to get up and scrub that oven?' I gained a different perspective on the nature of work. To this day, I think of that experience every time the oven needs cleaning."

She continues: "An unusual blessing came to me in having my mother available. She listened patiently to my early adolescent concerns and questions. She made me feel like the most important and interesting person in the world. She was *always* HOME—attentive, interested, and always available."

Her mother died the spring of her senior year of high school. She relates:

"One of the hardest moments in my young life was the day I returned home from school to an empty house and walked down that long hallway to her bedroom. My built-in counselor and confidante was no longer there, but she had given me those eternal, intangible gifts of love, wisdom, and acceptance. I will be forever grateful for her goodness."

This strong woman, though physically helpless, had the *power* to love, to motivate, to inspire, to perpetuate righteousness, to do good.

My plea for each of us is to recognize that God has given each of us power—the power to act, to choose, to serve, to love, and to accomplish *much good.* Perhaps it is time to take control of ourselves. Our prophet, Gordon B. Hinckley, has said, "Be faithful . . . do good." He has told us: "We have nothing to fear. God is at the helm. . . . He will shower down blessings upon those who walk in obedience to His commandments" ("This Is the Work of the Master," *Ensign,* May 1995, 71).

———

See Janette Hales Beckham, "The Power of Goodness," Ensign, *November 1995, 11.*

CROSSING THE FINISH LINE

~

Stephen D. Nadauld

Some years ago, while I was serving as a young bishop, we held a ward social around a swimming pool near the apartment where most of the ward members lived. I was introduced to a new member of the ward—a young woman by the name of Carol. Carol had cerebral palsy. She walked with great difficulty; her hands were crippled. Her kind and dear face was also affected, as was her speech. But as I would come to understand, to know Carol was to love her.

I had only to wait a few minutes to begin learning the great lesson she would teach. While we were talking, we watched a tall, very athletic young man dive off the diving board and seem to injure himself slightly. He got out of the pool, holding his neck,

———

Stephen D. Nadauld, a professor at the Marriott School of Management at Brigham Young University, has served as a member of the Second Quorum of the Seventy. He and his wife, Margaret D. Nadauld, who has served as Young Women general president, are the parents of seven children.

and went and sat under a tree. I watched as Carol struggled to prepare a plate of food and with great difficulty delivered it to him—a guileless act of service, of "good works." Carol's good works became a legend. She cared for the sick; she took food to the hungry; she drove people places; she comforted; she lifted; she blessed.

I walked with her one day on the sidewalk that passed through the apartment complex where she lived. From the windows, from the balconies, from the porches came cries of "Hi, Carol!" and "How are you doing, Carol?" and "Come up and see us, Carol!" Occasionally someone would say, "Oh, hi, Bishop." It was clear that Carol was loved and greatly accepted through her wonderful good works.

My most vivid recollection of Carol occurred in the spring of that year. The ward had agreed to participate in the stake five-kilometer fun run—an oxymoronic term, to be sure. Carol wanted to be with the rest of the ward members, but we didn't see how it would be possible. For her, just walking was a great difficulty. Nevertheless, she was determined. She struggled and trained each day to increase her endurance.

The race finished in the stadium. Two or three hundred of us were in the stands by the finish line, drinking juice and catching our breath. And then we remembered Carol—she was left somewhere back on the course. As we ran out the entrance of the stadium to find her, she came into view, struggling to breathe, barely able to walk, but determined to finish. As she started around the track toward the finish line, a wonderful thing happened. Suddenly the track was lined on both sides with hundreds of cheering friends. Others were running alongside to support and hold her up. Carol had finished the race.

One day each of us will cross the finish line. Will it likewise be to the cheers and encouragement of those we have loved and served? Hopefully it will be to the approbation of our Savior, who because of our faith and good works, will say, "Well done, thou good and faithful servant" (Matthew 25:21).

———

See Stephen D. Nadauld, "Put Your Faith to Work," New Era, September 1995, 4.

THE PROMISE OF JESUS

Spencer W. Kimball

I have learned that it is by serving that we learn how to serve. When we are engaged in the service of our fellowmen, not only do our deeds assist them, but we put our own problems in a fresher perspective. When we concern ourselves more with others, there is less time to be concerned with ourselves. In the midst of the miracle of serving, there is the promise of Jesus, that by losing ourselves, we find ourselves (Matthew 10:39).

Not only do we "find" ourselves in terms of acknowledging guidance in our lives, but the more we serve our fellowmen in appropriate ways, the more substance there is to our souls. We become more significant individuals as we serve others. We

---

Spencer W. Kimball was ordained an apostle in 1943 and sustained as president of the Church in 1973. He and his wife, Camilla Eyring Kimball, became the parents of four children. President Kimball died in 1985 at the age of ninety.

become more substantive as we serve others—indeed, it is easier to "find" ourselves because there is so much more of us to find!

George MacDonald observed that "it is by loving and not by being loved that one can come nearest to the soul of another" (*George MacDonald Anthology* [London: Geoffrey Bles, 1970]). Of course, we all need to be loved, but we must be giving and not always receiving if we want to have wholeness in our lives and a reinforced sense of purpose.

Our purpose is to become like God. God does nothing by chance but always by design as a loving father. You know his purpose. We have purpose also in our lives.

Surely such a loving Father in Heaven, who gave commandments to prevent human misery, will not forget the needs of each of his children. William Law observed:

"It is said that the very hairs of your head are all numbered; is it not to teach us that nothing, not the smallest things imaginable, happen to us by chance? But if the smallest things we can conceive of are declared to be under the divine direction, need we, or can we, be more plainly taught that the greatest things of life, such as the manner of our coming into the world, our parents, the time, and other circumstances of our birth and condition, are all according to the eternal purposes, direction, and appointment of divine Providence?" (*A Serious Call to a Devout and Holy Life* [Grand Rapids, Mich.: Sovereign Grace Publishers, 1971]).

God does notice us, and he watches over us. But it is usually through another person that he meets our needs. Therefore, it is vital that we serve each other in the kingdom. The people of the Church need each other's strength, support, and leadership in a community of believers as an enclave of disciples. In the Doctrine and Covenants we read about how important it is to "succor the weak, lift up the hands which hang down, and strengthen the feeble knees" (D&C 81:5). So often, our acts of service consist of simple encouragement or of giving mundane help with mundane tasks, but what glorious consequences can flow from mundane acts and from small but deliberate deeds!

———

See Spencer W. Kimball, "Small Acts of Service," Ensign, *December 1974, 2.*

Part Eight

We Love Life
and Learning

Be of Good Cheer

Jeanne B. Inouye

Our Heavenly Father knows and loves each of us; he knows the circumstances and challenges of our lives, and he will help us. The scriptures teach, "Wherefore, be of good cheer, and do not fear, for I the Lord am with you, and will stand by you" (D&C 68:6).

One thing I have learned is that motherhood entails difficult decisions. When our first child was born, I had been working for about twelve years, first as a teacher and later as a lawyer. I wondered whether to continue working. President Kimball, who was then the prophet, had counseled the sisters of the Church: "Some women, because of circumstances beyond their control, must work. We understand that. . . . Do not, however, make the mistake of being drawn off into secondary tasks which will cause the neglect

---

Jeanne Bryan Inouye has served as a member of the Relief Society general board and as chair of the BYU Women's Conference. She and her husband, Dillon K. Inouye, are the parents of two children.

of your eternal assignments such as giving birth to and rearing the spirit children of our Father in Heaven. Pray carefully over all your decisions" ("The Role of Righteous Women," *Ensign,* November 1979, 103).

I took this counsel seriously. I knew that I had to decide whether I was among those who must work. After praying earnestly about the matter, I sought a priesthood blessing from my husband. The blessing promised that I would be able to make a decision that would be good for our family but did not indicate what the decision should be. I tried to foresee the effect my decision would have on my husband, my children, and me and to listen for inspiration. My choice was to become a full-time homemaker.

I have not regretted that decision. I have loved being home with the children, watching them grow, and helping them learn. But I remain aware that a time may come when I must provide for my family. Having tried to make a wise decision and to do those things I can to maintain employable skills, I feel I must and can trust the Lord to help me should such a need arise.

Formulating priorities is an ongoing process for us all. Sisters throughout the Church, many in circumstances far more difficult than mine, have prayerfully considered the counsel of the prophets and sought the guidance of the Holy Ghost as they too have endeavored to make wise decisions regarding the well-being of their families. And though their decisions have been inevitably varied and diverse, and sometimes misunderstood by others, I believe that they too must and can trust the Lord to help them fulfill their responsibilities.

When we have been honest with ourselves and humble before the Lord in decisions about work and in the myriad decisions involved in mothering, we can go forward with courage. "For God hath not given us the spirit of fear; but of power, and of love, and of a sound mind" (2 Timothy 1:7).

As I have attempted to establish priorities, I have learned that we may almost always have too much to do. As a mother at home with only two children, I have too much to do. How much greater the demands are for women who work outside the home or whose families are large or who are parenting their children alone! As I think about our time constraints, I conclude that God has not intended that we should be able to do everything we would like to do. If there were not more to do than we are individually capable of doing, we wouldn't have to make choices and we would never realize what we value most.

It is often difficult to know what the most important things are. We are blessed to raise our children in a time when the gospel has been restored and when God has called prophets to help us with decision making.

I bear testimony of his love and interest in helping us, of the accessibility of his guidance through prophets and prayer, and of his kindness and forgiveness for the errors we may make. As mothers in Zion and as sisters in the gospel of Jesus Christ, we are on the Lord's errand. We may "be of good cheer," for he will be with us and stand by us.

———

See Jeanne Inouye, "Be of Good Cheer," Ensign, *November 1993, 96.*

"Dost Thou Love Life?"

Mary Ellen Edmunds

Time is a gift. It's a gift from God. We can't demand more, and we can't insist on less. We can't buy more, and we can't sell any (otherwise, it wouldn't really be a gift). Everyone in the world receives the same amount of time every day.

Benjamin Franklin asked: "Dost thou love life? Then do not squander time, for that is the stuff life is made of" (*The Oxford Dictionary of Quotations*, 3d ed. [Oxford: Oxford University Press, 1979], 218).

Time is our *life*—it's our *day* to prepare to be with God forever and ever. Time is given to us for that preparation, for repenting and forgiving and trying to be good and do good. Alma taught his son Corianton, further, "that there was a time granted unto

---

Mary Ellen Edmunds has served as director of training at the Missionary Training Center in Provo, Utah, and as a member of the Relief Society general board. She has taught in the College of Nursing at Brigham Young University and filled proselyting and welfare missions in Asia and Africa.

man . . . a probationary time, a time to repent and serve God" (Alma 42:4).

One of our challenges is to figure out which are the most important things in our life—where we should be putting our time and our energy and our other resources—right now, in this season of our lives. President Ezra Taft Benson taught us that "when we put God first, all other things fall into their proper place or drop out of our lives. Our love of the Lord will govern the . . . demands on our time, the interests we pursue, and the order of our priorities" ("We Bear Witness of Him," *Ensign*, May 1988, 4).

We have lots of chances to choose among a lot of things that are good, enjoyable, important, and exciting, not just between good and bad. If it were always a choice of doing good or bad, well, I'd still have a hard time sometimes, but mostly it is a choice between a lot of things which are good, important, valuable, and enjoyable.

Elder Neal A. Maxwell said: "The highest challenge we have in mortality is to use our free agency well, making right choices in the interplay of time and talents. Time is one of the blessings we are given" (*Deposition of a Disciple* [Salt Lake City: Deseret Book, 1976], 68).

How long has it been since you walked anywhere slowly, just thinking and feeling? Or went outside and looked at the stars?

Or watched the sun rise or set? Or played in the sandpile with a child, or laughed at the jokes from *Boys' Life?* Just being busy is not a sign that time is being used well.

In Mosiah 4:27, King Benjamin is teaching his people about helping and sharing: "And see that all these things are done in wisdom and order; for it is not requisite that a man should run faster than he has strength. And again, it is expedient that he should be diligent, that thereby he might win the prize; therefore, all things must be done in order."

Put *you* in that verse. We are told to liken the scriptures to ourselves, so put your name or your circumstance in the verse. Let's see how it might read: "And see that all these things are done in wisdom and order; for it is not requisite that a [mother of young children] should run faster than [she] has strength [amen!]. All things must be done in order." *You* fill in that blank: wife of the bishop, caretaker of aging parents, Relief Society president, mother of a child with a disability, woman who has to search for water and fuel every single day, full-time student, single parent, and on and on. (And you're sitting there thinking, *Well, I wonder which five I should put in my blank!)*

I am convinced that our Heavenly Father is aware of the season you are in. He is not just aware of what that season is; he understands it. He will not ask us to do anything stupid, anything that doesn't really matter. And our burdens will never be heavier than we can bear if we let him help and let others help.

I pray that we will live as happily and positively and enthusiastically as we possibly can the great plan of happiness, the gospel of Jesus Christ; that we will do as much as we possibly can, in any season in which we find ourselves; that we will use this precious time that our Heavenly Father has given us, this day of our lives, to do all we can to be more like him, closer to him, and to build up and defend the kingdom of God.

———

See Mary Ellen Edmunds, "It's About Time," Every Good Thing *(Salt Lake City: Deseret Book, 1998), 250.*

LET US REJOICE

Patricia P. Pinegar

While we were serving a mission in England, our seventeen-year-old son, Cory, was killed in a car accident. We were able to come home to Utah for his funeral, and then we immediately returned to England to finish our mission. It was a very tender time for our entire family.

The difficult experience of my son's death helped me identify and rejoice in the blessings of peace, hope, and direction—blessings that all who truly accept and live the gospel of Jesus Christ may enjoy. I can bear witness to the words of Elder Richard G. Scott: "Please learn that as you wrestle with a challenge and feel sadness because of it, you can simultaneously have peace and rejoicing" ("Trust in the Lord," *Ensign,* November 1995, 17).

Patricia P. Pinegar has served as Primary general president. She and her husband, Ed J. Pinegar, have filled missions together in England and at the Missionary Training Center in Provo, Utah. They are the parents of eight children.

What are some specific things we can do to have these blessings of peace, hope, and direction in our lives? May I share with you three things that have helped me.

First, we must have complete trust in our Father's plan of happiness and our Savior's part in that plan. Trusting in his plan gave me peace during the time following our son's death. I knew where our son was, and I knew Heavenly Father loved him. I had a perfect hope that because of the Savior's atonement Cory lived and we would be together again as an eternal family. I also had direction. I knew what I needed to do and what our family needed to do to be together forever.

The second thing that has helped me receive these blessings is the principle of courageous obedience. I am so grateful for God's gift of laws and commandments. Peace, hope, and direction are outcomes of striving to live the teachings of Jesus and obeying his laws and commandments. The scriptures teach, "Great peace have they which love thy law" (Psalm 119:165). They also teach that "he who doeth the works of righteousness shall receive his reward, even peace in this world, and eternal life in the world to come" (D&C 59:23). Obedience to these laws gives us peace, hope, and direction.

The third thing we can do to receive these blessings of peace, hope, and direction is to learn to respond to the promptings of the

Holy Ghost and acknowledge to the Lord our gratitude for this great gift.

Let us rejoice in the blessings of peace, hope, and direction, blessings that so many of our Father's children do not enjoy. I acknowledge the goodness and kindness of my Savior in every part of my life. The blessings of peace, hope, and direction that I have identified are only three of the many ways my life is blessed because of the gospel of Jesus Christ.

———

See Patricia P. Pinegar, "Peace, Hope, and Direction," Ensign, November 1999, 67.

Part Nine

We Stand for
Truth and
Righteousness

Press Forward with Steadfastness in Christ

Ardeth G. Kapp

Can we press forward with steadfastness in Christ having a perfect brightness of hope and a love of God and all men? The words of Nephi are very clear, "Ye [meaning you and me] must press forward" (2 Nephi 31:20).

Our Savior marked the path and led the way. We have entered the gate through the waters of baptism. We have received the Holy Ghost. We are on the path (2 Nephi 31:5). Our Father in Heaven wants us to be happy, very happy. He is our Father. The great plan of happiness of which Alma speaks (Alma 42) is God's plan for us. Not happiness in the way we might commonly think of happiness, but rather eternal happiness with all that the Father has and with our families together forever. It is this happiness that the Savior has made possible for us.

Ardeth Greene Kapp has served as general president of Young Women. A popular teacher, speaker, and writer, she and her husband, Heber B. Kapp, have served as matron and president of the Cardston Alberta Temple.

The Savior went all the way, through the agony of the Garden of Gethsemane, taking upon himself the sins of the world, to the cross where even in the last moment of his suffering, he prayed for his crucifiers. He died on the cross. He gave his life for us. Yes, this is what he did for you and for me. Is it asking too much for us to press forward with steadfastness? All the way? Every day?

When we determine to take a stand and commit to go the whole way, our whole life, our Father in Heaven will be with us the whole way, our whole life. Not just our immediate concerns, our temporary hurts and our pains, but our whole lifetime experience. The writings of C. S. Lewis suggest this idea: You know what it is like when you go to the dentist to get rid of a toothache? That's all you really want—get rid of the ache. But he won't stop there. He grinds and grinds until the decay is removed. Lewis says, "This Helper who will, in the long run, be satisfied with nothing less than absolute perfection, will also be delighted with the first feeble, stumbling effort you make tomorrow to do the simplest duty" (*Mere Christianity* [New York: Macmillan, 1952], 171–72).

When we press forward with steadfastness in Christ with a perfect brightness of hope, our lives have meaning. We begin not only to look but also to see, not only to touch but also to feel, not only to talk but also to communicate. Our otherwise routine activities can become an offering on the altar of God. We don't just serve, we nurture. We don't just take a loaf of bread, we share the bread of life. We're not just teaching a class, we're changing a life. Our gospel study is not to just know about Him but to know Him and strive to become like Him, filled with the love of God. Our lives have meaning and purpose.

We must keep the vision of the tree of life, the love of God, else we can become weary, even in well doing, and find ourselves surrounded by the mists of darkness in our exhaustion. With a firm grip on the iron rod but without the vision of the tree of life, we might be focused on the blisters on our hands and forget the hands scarred with nail prints. It is our vision of what we are working for, what we are living for, and what we want to happen in our lives that elevates us to a higher level of living because it gives meaning to everything we are doing.

"Ye must press forward . . . in Christ" (2 Nephi 31:20). We are women of covenant, we have taken upon us his name, to always remember him and keep his commandments, that we may always have his spirit to be with us. Elder Bruce R. McConkie explains, "There is no price too high, no labor too onerous, no struggle too severe, no sacrifice too great, if out of it all we receive and enjoy the gift of the Holy Ghost" (*A New Witness for the Articles of Faith* [Salt Lake City: Deseret Book, 1985], 253).

"Wherefore, if ye shall press forward feasting upon the words of Christ, and endure to the end, behold thus saith the Father: Ye shall have eternal life" (2 Nephi 31:20).

————

See Ardeth G. Kapp, "Pressing Forward," Arise and Shine Forth *(Salt Lake City: Deseret Book, 2001), 35.*

BUILT UPON THE ROCK

~⌐

Patricia T. Holland

This is the voice of Helaman to his sons Nephi and Lehi: "Remember, remember that it is upon the rock of our Redeemer, who is Christ, the Son of God, that ye must build your foundation; that when the devil shall send forth his mighty winds, yea, his shafts in the whirlwind, yea, when all his hail and his mighty storm shall beat upon you, it shall have no power over you to drag you down to the gulf of misery and endless wo, because of the rock upon which ye are built" (Helaman 5:12).

I assume you won't think me too bold or off-base if I say that when the winds blow and the sea is storm tossed, we must not give in to self-pity. God is with us; Christ is our sure foundation; there is a safe haven ahead. We simply have to remember that in this mortal journey, all learning, all personal growth, all spiritual

---

Patricia Terry Holland has served as first counselor in the Young Women general presidency. She and her husband, Elder Jeffrey R. Holland of the Quorum of the Twelve Apostles, are the parents of three children.

refinement carry with them the possibility of a little motion sickness. No one—not even the Saints, maybe especially not the Saints—are immune from such challenges. No one escapes God's refining hand. Our trials offer a training ground for godhood. Without some moments in darkness, would we ever cherish the light? Without confronting some doubt, would we ever recognize and cling to faith?

I don't pretend to have any prepackaged solutions to individual sorrows, but I have come to say that I love you and that I know some very basic things to be true. God can mend our broken hearts. Indeed, I believe it is through the cracks of a broken heart that God sheds his purest and most illuminating light to the soul.

My entire message is simply this: "Please trust lovingly in the goodness of God. He will honor the covenants you have made with him!" Glorious and glimmering promises await you if you will but trust in him. Illuminating secrets, clearly revealed, are awaiting you—the wonder of rewards found in "small round coins thrown by those who wished for something else." You are God's child. He loves you—and he will never stop loving you. You are still being formed and transformed at his tender hand. Though his molding requires that we walk through the valley of the shadow of death, he has provided for you a pathway of peace. Even through the darkest of shadows, you can walk in comfort and consolation if you lovingly trust God. Remember your baptism. Remember the sacrament table. Remember the temple. Remember an entire theology built upon covenants. Well did Pierre Teilhard de Chardin write, "Not everything is immediately good to those who seek God; but everything is capable of becoming good" (*The Divine Milieu* [New York: Harper & Row, 1960], 86). Things are *made* good through the power of covenants.

"Only God is able. It is faith in him that we must rediscover. With this faith we can transform bleak and desolate valleys into sunlit paths of joy and bring new light into the dark caverns of pessimism. Is someone here moving toward the twilight of life and fearful of that which we call death? Why be afraid? God is able. Is someone here on the brink of despair because of the death of a loved one, the breaking of a marriage, or the waywardness of a child? Why despair? God is able to give you the power to endure that which cannot be changed. Is someone here anxious because of bad health? Why be anxious? Come what may, God is able" (Martin Luther King Jr., *Strength to Love* [Cleveland, Ohio: Collins, 1963], 112).

You may be asking, "How do I do this? How do I make the transition from reading powerful testimonies in the scriptures, only to go out into that world of woe that confronts us all from time to time?" My answer is not new, and it has everything to do with covenants—the promise that if we will remember something as fundamental as our baptismal, sacramental, and temple covenants, we will carry an inner peace that God is with us. Knowing precisely the doubts and difficult moments all of us would face, the great Jehovah said to the children of Israel, "For I know the things that come into your mind, every one of them. . . . I will be to [you] as a little sanctuary. . . . I will put a new spirit within you" (Ezekiel 11: 5–19). When difficult times come, when we realize things are not good the way they are, we trust in God, who can provide a new spirit. That is the power of covenant making and covenant keeping.

———

See Patricia T. Holland, "God's Covenant of Peace," The Arms of His Love (Salt Lake City: Deseret Book, 2000), 365.

Choose Righteousness

Sharon G. Larsen

"Choose you this day whom ye will serve; . . . but *as for me and my house, we will serve the Lord*" (Joshua 24:15; italics added).

President Boyd K. Packer is a modern-day Joshua. He said, "I am not ashamed to say that . . . I want to be good. . . . This was established between me and the Lord so that I knew that He knew which way I had committed my agency. I went before Him and in essence said, 'I'm not neutral, and You can do with me what you want. . . . You don't have to take anything from me because I give it to You—everything, all I own, all I am.' And that makes the difference" (*"That All May Be Edified": Talks, Sermons and*

Sharon G. Larsen has served on the Young Women general board and as second counselor in the Young Women general presidency. A writer and schoolteacher, she has also taught seminary and institute. She and her husband, Ralph T. Larsen, are the parents of two children.

Commentary by Boyd K. Packer [Salt Lake City: Deseret Book, 1982], 272).

When we use our agency to wholly and freely turn ourselves over to God, we will rise as His—free and unburdened.

The cycle of choice, action, consequences, choice, action, consequences, affects our character and our life experiences. Every day and every decision determines the next. In time we will look back at what may seem like disconnected, independent pieces of our lives and better understand what God is trying to make of us. You remember the analogy quoted by C. S. Lewis: "Imagine yourself as a living house. God comes in to rebuild that house. At first, perhaps, you can understand what He is doing. He is getting the drains right and stopping the leaks in the roof and so on: you knew that those jobs needed doing and so you are not surprised. But presently he starts knocking the house about in a way that hurts abominably and does not seem to make sense. What on earth is He up to? The explanation is that He is building quite a different house from the one you thought of—throwing out a new wing here, putting on an extra floor there, running up towers, making courtyards. You thought you were going to be made into a decent little cottage: but He is building a palace" (*Mere Christianity* [New York: Macmillan, 1952], 174).

God can make much more out of our lives than we can—if we will let Him.

It is being able to choose righteously that helps us to grow up. Using agency, in harmony with God's will, helps us learn about ourselves. It teaches us what the Lord already knows about us. He asked Adam where he was because *Adam* needed to know where he was (Genesis 3:9; Moses 4:15).

We have repeated the second Article of Faith since Primary days. If we really believe we will be punished for our own sins, why aren't we better than we are? Obedience to God's laws frees us spiritually.

Viktor Frankl was a psychiatrist who endured years of unspeakable horror in Nazi death camps. He said, "Everything can be taken from a man but one thing: the last of the human freedoms—to choose one's attitude in any given set of circumstances, to choose one's own way" (*Man's Search for Meaning* [New York: Washington Square, 1984], 87).

It takes faith to choose the good. Exercising faith in the Lord and His plan for us is spiritual calisthenics. We have opportunities every day to improve that skill so we will not be deceived. As women of God, we can feel His love and His strength every day. Even though we are trying to do the best we can, we all slip and pick ourselves up and try again, and the Lord is there to dust us off. Some are carrying heavy, heavy burdens. None of us is free from tribulation or weighty loads, but I testify (because I know) that He *will* make us strong to carry the weight placed upon us. Let Him heal our broken hearts and broken dreams.

President George Q. Cannon reminds us: "No matter how serious the trial, how deep the distress, how great the affliction, [God] will never desert us. He never has, and He never will. . . . We have made Him our friend, by obeying His gospel; and He will stand by us. . . . We shall emerge from all [our] trials and difficulties the better and purer for them, if we only trust in our God and keep His commandments" ("Freedom of the Saints," in *Collected Discourses,* comp. Brian H. Stuy, 5 vols. [Burbank, Calif.: B. H. Publishing, 1988], 2:185).

We can arise as women of God when we choose to trust Him and keep His commandments.

See Sharon G. Larsen, "The One Who Keeps His Promises," Arise and Shine Forth *(Salt Lake City: Deseret Book, 2001), 301.*

STAND FIRM

~

Virginia U. Jensen

To stand firm we must know in the core of our souls that the Lord will be our support if we stand firmly planted on the rock of our Redeemer. To maintain a firm stance for ourselves and help others stand firm, the message of the restored gospel must be firmly planted in our hearts and taught in our homes. In your own homes, give your children and loved ones the spiritual armor they will need as they leave you each day and venture away from the safe fortress of your home. Teach your loved ones how to draw upon the powers of heaven through fasting and prayer. Teach them that keeping the Sabbath day holy will insulate them from the world. Teach them to be obedient. Teach them to seek God's approval, not man's. Teach them that the only route back to our

---

Virginia U. Jensen has served as first counselor in the Relief Society general presidency. A homemaker who enjoys gardening, grandchildren, and family activities, she and her husband, J. Rees Jensen, are the parents of four children.

heavenly home is by loving and following the Savior and by making and keeping sacred covenants and commandments. The truths of the gospel and knowledge of the plan of salvation are weapons your family members can use for victory over Satan's evil forces.

In our roles as wives, mothers, grandmothers, sisters, and aunts, we must stand firm as role models. Because we love them, we want to give our family members a strong, righteous pattern to follow. In everything we do and say, in how we dress, in how we spend our time, in all the choices we make, we demonstrate what we believe, and that becomes their pattern to follow.

Lucy Mack Smith, mother of the Prophet Joseph Smith, recorded in her history that in the spring of 1803 she and her husband were much concerned about religion. She writes of her own search for truth, "I retired to a grove not far distant, where I prayed to the Lord . . . that the true gospel might be presented" (*History of Joseph Smith*, ed. Preston Nibley [Salt Lake City: Bookcraft, 1958], 43). Does that sound familiar?

Seventeen years later, in the spring of 1820, the Prophet Joseph Smith, in search of truth, "came to the determination to 'ask of God.'" So "I retired to the woods to make the attempt" (Joseph Smith–History 1:13–14).

Is it a coincidence that both mother and son chose a grove of trees as the place to ask God to reveal truth to them? Joseph's prayer blessed the entire world through the restoration of the gospel of Jesus Christ. The righteous example set by a woman who stands firm in faith blesses countless others.

As much as I love being a wife and mother, I acknowledge it isn't always easy. I can appreciate the feelings expressed by a grade-school girl when my friend, her teacher, asked the class to write letters to God. Sharon said, "Dear God, I bet it's very hard for you to love everyone in the world. There are only five people in my family, and I just can't do it." In like manner, I'm certain my family members could tell you it's not always easy for them to love me. However, I agree with Elder Loren C. Dunn, who said, "There can be nothing more precious or enduring than the family" ("Our Precious Families," *Ensign,* November 1974, 9). In spite of how difficult family life can be at times, the work we do in our families is of the utmost importance. When you are discouraged and things in your family are not going the way you wanted them to, stand firm with faith and say like another young schoolgirl in her letter to God, "Dear God, I'm doing the very best I can." Don't allow the difficulties inherent in family life to unduly discourage you or to impact the love which we can share in families.

Let us arm ourselves with faith and stand firm in our convictions. Let us never forget that we are building a foundation for and with our family upon the rock of our Redeemer. Let us put our hand into God's hand. With the Lord's help, we can build homes that are a righteous fortress.

———

See Virginia U. Jensen, "Stand Firm," Ensign, November 2001, 93–96.

DISTINCT AND DIFFERENT

Spencer W. Kimball

We know that God is perfect in his love for each and all of us as his spirit children. When we know these truths, my sisters and associates in this divine cause, it should help us greatly as we all experience much less than perfect love and perfect justice in the world. If, in the short term, we are sometimes dealt with insensitively and thoughtlessly by others, by imperfect men and women, it may still cause us pain, but such pain and disappointment are not the whole of life. The ways of the world will not prevail, for the ways of God will triumph.

We had full equality as his spirit children. We have equality as recipients of God's perfected love for each of us. The late Elder John A. Widtsoe wrote: "The place of woman in the Church is to

---

Spencer W. Kimball was ordained an apostle in 1943 and sustained as president of the Church in 1973. He and his wife, Camilla Eyring Kimball, became the parents of four children. President Kimball died in 1985 at the age of ninety.

walk beside the man, not in front of him nor behind him. In the Church there is full equality between man and woman. The gospel, which is the only concern of the Church, was devised by the Lord for men and women alike" (*Improvement Era*, March 1942, 161).

Within those great assurances, however, our roles and assignments differ. These are eternal differences—with women being given many tremendous responsibilities of motherhood and sisterhood and men being given the tremendous responsibilities of fatherhood and the priesthood—but the man is not without the woman nor the woman without the man in the Lord (1 Corinthians 11:11). Both a righteous man and a righteous woman are a blessing to all those their lives touch.

Remember, in the world before we came here, faithful women were given certain assignments while faithful men were foreordained to certain priesthood tasks. While we do not now remember the particulars, this does not alter the glorious reality of what we once agreed to. You are accountable for those things which long ago were expected of you just as are those we sustain as prophets and apostles!

Even though the eternal roles of men and women differ, this leaves much to be done by way of parallel personal development—for both men and women. In this connection, I stress the deep need each woman has to study the scriptures. We want our homes to be blessed with sister scriptorians—whether you are single or married, young or old, widowed or living in a family.

Regardless of your particular circumstances, as you become more and more familiar with the truths of the scriptures, you will be more and more effective in keeping the second great commandment, to love your neighbor as yourself. Become scholars of the scriptures—not to put others down, but to lift them up! After all, who has any greater need to "treasure up" (D&C 6:20) the truths of the gospel (on which they may call in their moments of need) than do women and mothers who do so much nurturing and teaching?

Seek excellence in all your righteous endeavors and in all aspects of your lives.

Bear in mind, dear sisters, that the eternal blessings which are yours through membership in The Church of Jesus Christ of Latter-day Saints are far, far greater than any other blessings you could possibly receive. No greater recognition can come to you in this world than to be known as a woman of God. No greater status can be conferred upon you than being a daughter of God who experiences true sisterhood, wifehood, and motherhood, or other tasks which influence lives for good.

How special it is for Latter-day Saint women to be given the lofty assignments they have been given by our Father in Heaven, especially those of you who have been privileged to be born in this part of this last dispensation. Let other women pursue heedlessly what they perceive as their selfish interests. You can be a much-needed force for love and truth and righteousness on this planet. Let others selfishly pursue false values, but God has given to you the tremendous tasks of *nurturing* families, friends, and neighbors, just as men are to *provide*. But *both* husband and wife are to be parents!

Finally, my dear sisters, may I suggest to you something that has not been said before or at least not in quite this way. Much of the major growth that is coming to the Church in the last days will come because many of the good women of the world (in whom there is often such an inner sense of spirituality) will be drawn to the Church in large numbers. This will happen to the degree that the women of the Church reflect righteousness and articulateness in their lives and to the degree that the women of the Church are seen as distinct and different—in happy ways—from the women of the world.

See Spencer W. Kimball, "Role of Righteous Women," Ensign, November 1979, 102.

Part Ten

We Sustain the
Priesthood as the Authority
of God on Earth

WOMEN AND THE PRIESTHOOD

◯

Ardeth G. Kapp

President Spencer W. Kimball, speaking to the women of the Church, addressed us with these stirring words: "To be a righteous woman is a glorious thing in any age. To be a righteous woman during the winding-up scenes on this earth, before the second coming of our Savior, is an especially noble calling. [Note that he speaks of our *calling*.] The righteous woman's strength and influence today can be tenfold what it might be in more tranquil times" (*My Beloved Sisters* [Salt Lake City: Deseret Book, 1979], 17). We do not live in tranquil times, but they are *our* times—wonderful times as we consider the Lord's plan and system relating to women leaders and priesthood authority.

The prophet Joel recorded the promise of the Lord: "I will pour out my spirit upon all flesh; and your sons and your

_____

Ardeth Greene Kapp has served as general president of Young Women. A popular teacher, speaker, and writer, she and her husband, Heber B. Kapp, have served as matron and president of the Cardston Alberta Temple.

daughters shall prophesy, . . . your young men shall see visions: and also upon the servants and upon the handmaids in those days will I pour out my spirit" (Joel 2:28–29). I bear testimony of this promise. More is required of us as women than simply to wait "in some back room" until called upon.

If there is any question about the worth of a righteous woman's influence, her value, and her insights, consider the words of President Hinckley, speaking to the women of the Church: "I feel to invite women everywhere to rise to the great potential within you. I do not ask that you reach beyond your capacity. I hope you will not nag yourselves with thoughts of failure. I hope you will not try to set goals far beyond your capacity to achieve. I hope you will simply do what you can do in the best way you know. If you do so, you will witness miracles come to pass" (*Teachings of Gordon B. Hinckley* [Salt Lake City: Deseret Book, 1997], 696).

He reminds us: "We are here to assist our Father in His work and His glory, 'to bring to pass the immortality and eternal life of man' (Moses 1:39). Your obligation is as serious in your sphere of responsibility as is my obligation in my sphere. No calling in this church is small or of little consequence" ("This Is the Work of the Master," *Ensign*, May 1995, 71).

We are called to take a stand, to contribute, to be accountable. This is not a time to ride the tide or to retreat. "They who are not for me are against me, saith our God" (2 Nephi 10:16). This is not a tranquil time but rather a time to participate in a meaningful way in councils, in our communities, and in our individual spheres of influence. And how broad is this influence? It begins in the home and moves out well beyond the walls of our homes, beyond the margins of our fields and the borders of our towns and cities.

When we as women attune our ears to the words of prophets as from the voice of the Lord himself (D&C 1:38), we are lifted, elevated, and magnified in our possibilities and opportunities. From our homes will come children who have been nurtured and prepared as leaders for generations to come. There is nowhere that our influence is more important to the Lord's work than in our homes, but it must not stop there. A righteous woman's influence extends beyond the home.

———

See Ardeth G. Kapp, "Women as Leaders," May Christ Lift Thee Up (Salt Lake City: Deseret Book, 1999), 288.

SUSTAINING AND BEING SUSTAINED BY THE PRIESTHOOD

Marie K. Hafen

Because of the Restoration, the priesthood—the power and authority of God—is once more on the earth. That power sustains me in every need and mood of my life. It also offers me the ordinances, the blessings, and the teachings of truth that give meaning to all I care about now and to all I hope for in the future.

Because of the priesthood keys given to Joseph Smith and his divinely appointed successors, every worthy member of the Church has access to the blessings of the priesthood. Under the hands of authorized priesthood representatives, each member may receive such glorious blessings as baptism for the remission of sins, the gift of the Holy Ghost, healings, patriarchal blessings, marriage,

---

Marie Kartchner Hafen has served on the Young Women general board and on the board of the Deseret News. *She has taught writing and Shakespeare courses at Brigham Young University and BYU–Idaho. She and her husband, Bruce C. Hafen, a member of the First Quorum of the Seventy, are the parents of seven children.*

and the holy endowment of the temple. Through the ordinances of the priesthood, the very "power of godliness is manifest" to us (D&C 84:20). Because of this divine power, we may be healed, inspired, forgiven, and sanctified.

When we sustain the priesthood as it is defined in this sense, we are doing more than respecting the Lord's servants who administer the ordinances, important as that is. We are also honoring our sacred priesthood covenants and reflecting profound gratitude for our priesthood blessings.

Elder Bruce R. McConkie spoke in the October 1977 general conference about ten blessings of the priesthood. Women, both single and married, can partake of almost all of these blessings by virtue of their Church membership, which is built upon the foundation of priesthood authority. Among the list Elder McConkie discussed are these stirring possibilities:

- receiving the fulness of the everlasting gospel;
- enjoying the gifts of the Spirit;
- becoming sanctified, exalted, and given the gift of eternal life in the presence of God;
- representing Jesus Christ in administering salvation to mankind;
- having the opportunity of eternal marriage and exaltation in

the celestial kingdom ("The Ten Blessings of the Priesthood," *Ensign,* November 1977, 33–35).

Most of these blessings are the personal, spiritual kind, relating to the process of individual perfection in a close relationship with God. They include the right to behold visions and receive revelation, for the Lord "imparteth his word by angels unto men, yea, not only men but women also" (Alma 32:23). Also included are spiritual gifts such as faith, the testimony of Christ, wisdom, tongues, prophecy, and personal revelation. Elder Dallin H. Oaks explained, "These gifts come by the power of the Holy Ghost and . . . are available to every member of the Church, male and female" ("Spiritual Gifts," *Ensign,* September 1986, 72).

Among the greatest of the priesthood blessings is the temple ordinance of eternal marriage. Unless we enter into this priesthood ordinance in this life or in the hereafter, we cannot receive exaltation. This privilege, though the ultimate blessing of the priesthood, is not available to a worthy holder of the priesthood unless he is sealed in eternal marriage to a woman who is as worthy as he is. How significant it is for our understanding of the interdependence and equality of men and women in the eyes of God to know that neither can achieve exaltation alone!

Both partners in an eternal marriage "sustain the priesthood" that sealed them by striving always to be faithful to each other and to the Lord.

All my experience teaches me that as I seek to sustain the priesthood, whether through loyalty to my husband, to my appointed leaders, or to my Savior, the priesthood sustains me, for the priesthood is the power of him who will not forsake me. Whether we are married or single, male or female, leaders or followers, if we sustain the priesthood by holding on our way as followers of Christ, "the priesthood will remain" with us (D&C 122:9).

See Marie K. Hafen, "Sustaining—and Being Sustained by—the Priesthood," Ensign, March 1987, 6.

WOMEN OF THE COVENANT

~

Elaine L. Jack

To be a woman of covenant is a sacred and holy responsibility. It is uniquely ours. It is not by chance that we are on the Lord's errand at this time. It is by choice that we came to this earth to follow the path of the Savior. At baptism, we covenanted, as did the Nephites at the waters of Mormon, to be called his people, to serve him, to keep his commandments, to stand as witnesses of God at all times and in all things and in all places (Mosiah 18:8–10). Indeed, we stand before the world today to rejoice—not in the power of men and women—but in the goodness of God.

Eliza R. Snow said: "We stand in a different position . . . ; we have made covenant with God, we understand his order" (*Millennial Star,* September 1871, 578). These covenants include

---

Elaine L. Jack has served as general president of the Relief Society and as matron of the Cardston Alberta Temple. A native of Canada, she attended the University of Utah as an English major. She and her husband, Joseph E. Jack, are the parents of four sons.

the counsel to Emma Smith recorded in the Doctrine and Covenants to "lay aside the things of this world, and seek for the things of a better" (D&C 25:10).

We have the blessings of the priesthood in these latter days to help us see clearly and act accordingly. As disciples of Christ, we are blessed with more than common sense, good ideas, and righteous inclinations. We must always remember that "Jesus Christ is the great High Priest of God; Christ is therefore the source of all true priesthood authority and power on this earth" (*Encyclopedia of Mormonism* [New York: Macmillan, 1992], 1133).

We know what it is to place our faith, our prayers, our confidence, and our esteem in those whom God has appointed to lead. The Lord has told us that "whether by mine own voice or by the voice of my servants, it is the same" (D&C 1:38).

I want you to know that I embrace the blessings that come from serving under the direction of leaders who hold the priesthood. We must stand united as a people for the Lord to call us one. Elder John A. Widtsoe spoke of men and women yoked together in their joint devotion to righteous principles when he said: "In the ordinances of the Priesthood man and woman share alike. . . . In the Church of Christ, woman is not an adjunct to, but an equal partner with man" (*Relief Society Magazine,* June-July 1943, 373).

Women and men have available every priesthood blessing essential for salvation—the blessings of being baptized, receiving the Holy Ghost, renewing our covenants through taking the sacrament, and making and keeping temple covenants. As women of covenant, we know and understand the guidance in the Doctrine and Covenants, which is counsel for women as well as for men: "Their hearts are set so much upon the things of this world, and aspire to the honors of men, that they do not learn this one lesson—. . . the powers of heaven cannot be controlled nor handled only upon the principles of righteousness" (D&C 121:35–36).

Look to the Lord for direction and guidance. We were reminded that each of us has the privilege to carefully and prayerfully seek the Lord's will, just for us, regarding life's challenges. This is God's plan, and it is not our prerogative to alter or tamper with it. I know that we, daughters of the Most High God, are here to do the Lord's will in an era most difficult, yet at a time that the angels of God rejoice in our efforts. I know that the Lord reigns supreme and that he has prepared a place for us in his kingdom on high. I know that as women of covenant we will choose that path to life eternal.

See Elaine L. Jack, "Ponder the Path of Thy Feet," Ensign, November 1993, 98.

WHAT IT MEANS TO SUSTAIN

Janette Hales Beckham

As you think of the word *sustaining,* ask yourself this question: Is sustaining the living prophets different from having a testimony that we have prophets? When we sustain, it means we *do* something about our belief. Our testimony of the prophet turns into action when we sustain him.

In general conference in October 1994, Elder David B. Haight said: "When we sustain the President of the Church by our uplifted hand, it not only signifies that we acknowledge before God that he is the rightful possessor of all the priesthood keys; it means that we covenant with God that we will abide by the direction and the counsel that comes through His prophet. It is a solemn covenant" ("Solemn Assemblies," *Ensign,* November 1994, 14–15).

Janette Hales Beckham has served as general president of Young Women. She and her late husband, Robert H. Hales, are the parents of five children. She married Raymond E. Beckham in 1995.

211

I pondered the words of Elder Haight. I considered the commitment I was making when I raised my hand and made a solemn covenant with God that I would sustain the prophet.

The following April, the members of the Church sustained President Gordon B. Hinckley as prophet, seer, and revelator and president of The Church of Jesus Christ of Latter-day Saints, with President Thomas S. Monson and President James E. Faust as his counselors. President Hinckley said at that conference: "The procedure of sustaining is much more than a ritualistic raising of the hand. It is a commitment to uphold, to support, to assist those who have been selected" ("This Work Is Concerned with People," *Ensign,* May 1995, 51). When we sustain, it affects our behavior. President Hinckley also quoted the Doctrine and Covenants, section 107, verse 22, where we are told that the First Presidency, or "three Presiding High Priests," are "appointed and ordained to that office, and upheld by the confidence, faith, and prayer of the church."

Surely we are standing as witnesses of God when we sustain his living prophets, especially when we know what it means to sustain. We will abide by the direction and counsel of the prophets. We indeed become witnesses when we make this solemn covenant.

As a young child, I believed we had a prophet and that he spoke the truth; but I'm not sure I understood that the prophet was speaking to me personally. When I was a young wife and mother, my husband spent two years in the air force. We lived in military housing on Long Island, New York. While tending our young children, I often visited with neighbors who had come from all over the country. One day as a neighbor and I were talking about our beliefs, she became curious about what was different about The Church of Jesus Christ of Latter-day Saints.

I told her briefly about the Restoration, and I explained that the restored Church of Jesus Christ has a living prophet today. This really seemed to pique her interest, and she wanted to know what the prophet had said. As I started to tell her about the Doctrine and Covenants and modern revelation, she said, "But what has he said lately?" I told her about general conference and that the Church had a monthly publication with a message from the prophet. Then she got really interested. I was so embarrassed to admit that I hadn't read the current message. She concluded our conversation by saying, "You mean you have a living prophet and you don't know what he said?" In that situation I hadn't shown what it meant to sustain.

When the prophets speak to us, it is as if our Heavenly Father is speaking to us. Doctrine and Covenants 1:38 states, "Whether by mine own voice or by the voice of my servants, it is the same."

Fortunately, in this day of satellites and other modern

technology, we can see and hear the prophet. We can read and reread his messages. It is my prayer that we will show by our behavior that we are a covenant people, that we sustain the living prophets.

———

See Janette Hales Beckham, "Sustaining the Living Prophets," Ensign, *May 1996, 84.*

A Prophet's Voice

Virginia U. Jensen

Prophets ancient and modern were and are giants of the Lord, chosen and ordained before they came to this earth. Our prophets are men whom the Lord has raised up specifically to preside over the Church for the particular time in which they have served. The Lord is working through the leaders of his Church today, just as he has always done in the past.

President Wilford Woodruff said, "If we had before us every revelation which God ever gave to man . . . and they were piled up here a hundred feet high, the Church and kingdom of God could not grow, in this or any other age of the world, without the living oracles of God" ("The Keys of the Kingdom," *Millennial Star* 51, 548).

Virginia U. Jensen has served as first counselor in the Relief Society general presidency. A homemaker who enjoys gardening, grandchildren, and family activities, she and her husband, J. Rees Jensen, are the parents of four children.

The Lord's will to Abraham was not sufficient for the people of Moses' time. The will of the Lord to Moses was not sufficient for the people of Isaiah's time. Different dispensations required different instructions. That is true today. The dispensation in which we now live is a dispensation into which the knowledge of all other dispensations of the gospel have merged. What a blessing it is for us to live in this time when the fulness of the gospel is ours to bless our lives.

The story is told of an event that happened in New York when President David O. McKay returned from a trip to Europe. "Arrangements had been made for pictures to be taken, but the regular photographer was unable to go, so in desperation the United Press picked their crime photographer—a man accustomed to the toughest type of work in New York. He went to the airport, stayed there two hours, and returned later from [the] dark room with a tremendous sheaf of pictures. He was supposed to take only two. His boss immediately chided him, 'What in the world are you wasting time and all those photographic supplies for?'

"The photographer replied very curtly, saying he would gladly pay for the extra materials, and they could even dock him for the extra time he took. . . . Several hours later the vice-president called him to his office, wanting to learn what happened. The crime photographer said, 'When I was a little boy, my mother used to read to me out of the Old Testament, and all my life I have wondered what a prophet of God must really look like. Well, today I found one' " (*Improvement Era,* February 1970, 72).

Do we fully appreciate what a wondrous blessing it is to each one of us that we have found our prophet? The ways in which our lives have been enriched by listening to our prophet's voice are numerous. We have a clearer picture of who we are and what we mean to our Father in Heaven. We have received commandments and counsel to guide us, reminders to keep us on the straight and narrow, and encouraging words to spur us on when we become disheartened or discouraged. If we listen to the voices of the world, we will be misled. But if we listen to the voice of the Lord through his living prophet and follow his counsel, we will never go astray.

God's message was never more clear and sure or safe and direct than when President Gordon B. Hinckley read, as part of his message at the general Relief Society meeting held September 23, 1995, the proclamation on the family ("The Family: A Proclamation to the World," *Ensign,* November 1995, 102). Look at the lessons God taught a floundering world through this proclamation: Marriage between a man and a woman is ordained of God. We are created in his image. Our gender was determined before we came to earth and is part of our eternal identity. We lived with him before we came to earth. God commanded us to bear children but warned that the powers of procreation were to be employed only within the sacred bonds of marriage. God tells us through his prophet that we have a solemn responsibility to love and care for each other as husband and wife and to rear our children in love and righteousness, to provide for their physical and spiritual needs. The family is ordained of God. Parents have specific duties and responsibilities—fathers preside, provide, and protect, and mothers nurture. In addition, the proclamation contains this very important warning—that those who abuse spouse or offspring, who fail to fulfill family responsibilities will stand accountable before God. Further, this warning—that the disintegration of the family will bring upon individuals, communities, and nations the calamities foretold by ancient and modern prophets. Brothers and sisters, we are in the midst of that reality at this very moment. It is the duty of all of us to protect and strengthen the family.

I invite you to "come, listen to a prophet's voice" (*Hymns* [Salt Lake City: The Church of Jesus Christ of Latter-day Saints, 1985], no. 21). The Prophet Joseph Smith established Relief Society as a result of a revelation from God, so that "knowledge and intelligence shall flow down from this time henceforth." Joseph Smith promised, "You will receive instructions through the order of the Priesthood which God has established, through the medium of those appointed to lead, guide and direct the affairs of the Church in this last dispensation" (*History of The Church of Jesus Christ of Latter-day Saints,* ed. B. H. Roberts, 2d ed. rev., 7 vols. [Salt Lake City: The Church of Jesus Christ of Latter-day Saints, 1932–51], 4:607).

In Relief Society, we are taught ways to protect and strengthen the family.

President Hinckley has said, "The best lies ahead. . . . If you will stay on the straight and narrow, the best lies ahead. It is a wonderful time to be alive. It's a great time to be a member of this Church when you can hold your head up without embarrassment and with some pride in this great latter-day work" (West High School seminary graduation, 14 May 1995; cited in *Church News,* 2 September 1995, 2).

"Come, listen to a prophet's voice," that you may know the will of God, that you may have his light to direct your path.

———

See Virginia U. Jensen, "'Come, Listen to a Prophet's Voice,'" Ensign, *November 1998, 12.*

Part Eleven

We Rejoice in the
Blessings of the Temple

The Wonder of Temples

Virginia H. Pearce

Temples are an expression of the Savior's love and mercy—his outstretched hand—offering us a way to return to the presence of the Father in spite of our sins and shortcomings. The ordinances of the temple invite us and all of our kindred dead to receive the fullness. When we have a temple, we have everything the Father has to offer us on this earth.

I am filled with the wonder of temple after temple being built and dedicated in great cities and isolated towns. Surely, they are evidence of the hastening of the work promised by the Lord (D&C 88:73). Temples fill our thoughts and actions. It is difficult to put into words the unity we feel as members of the Church as we play our part.

Think of the words associated with temples: *sacrifice, purity of*

_____

Virginia H. Pearce, who received a master's degree in social work from the University of Utah, has served as first counselor in the Young Women general presidency. She and her husband, James R. Pearce, are the parents of six children.

heart, preparation, protection, power. They are words that are prominent in the histories of our first temples in Kirtland and Nauvoo. Surely, they are still relevant to temples today.

Sacrifice. What does it mean to us? We aren't the women of Nauvoo sewing shirts for the men who worked on the temple. We don't spin, weave, or give crushed china to mix with the plaster in Kirtland. But we tithe our income. There is so much more about sacrifice in temple worship. Is there a more precious commodity in our day than time? Whether it be a temple trip requiring days or a drive across town with a total time of three hours—it is time, and as such, a personal sacrifice.

Purity of heart. It is impossible to talk about sacrifice without talking about purity of heart. A pure heart is both the antecedent and consequence of sacrifice. We make our sacrifices out of the purity of our hearts. We purify our hearts through sacrifice.

President Gordon B. Hinckley has said that we have not partaken of the gospel fully unless we have served vicariously for others. This work more nearly approaches the work of the Savior than any other. We give a gift without a possibility of receiving thanks—at least in this life—from the recipient. Doing work for the dead is a sacred and sanctifying work (*Teachings of Gordon B. Hinckley* [Salt Lake City: Deseret Book, 1997], 336). Yes, serving vicariously is a sacrifice that purifies our hearts.

Preparation. With our historical hindsight, we can surmise that the preliminary Kirtland endowment prepared the brethren to go forth and spread the gospel as missionaries. We might say that the endowment in Nauvoo prepared the Saints for their grueling exodus to the west. What does the endowment prepare you and me for? I don't know, but I have some ideas. I think that you might agree with me that each of us probably has a grueling experience or two in our future. More than one event or circumstance that will require vision and faith and eternal perspective. Eternal perspective is what the temple offers us—and it offers it to us again and again as we are given the privilege of hearing it not just once but time after time as we stand proxy for others. The temple is a constant refresher of the great and meaningful things of life. Do you think that eternal perspective kept the Saints going when they fled from Kirtland and Missouri and Nauvoo? It made all the difference. Do you think it makes a difference now? The more clear our understanding of the Big Picture, the more energy we will have to live the details. Temples are a constant refresher of the great and meaningful things of life—they help us to sift through the clutter. Do we need this in an age of information overload? I do.

Protection. We are prepared for the future as we understand more completely the Plan. This understanding offers us protection. What kind of protection? There is no limit, I believe. But certainly the knowledge and understanding offered us in the temple protect us from Satan's cunning traps. Our very worthiness to enter the house of the Lord indicates that we are protected from the ravages of drugs, alcohol, immorality, and other assaults. The temple recommend we carry is an indication of our faith and works—and faith and works bring with them their own blessings of protection.

Power. Our worthiness allows us in our extremities to call down the powers of heaven. We pause in the celestial room, hearts open in prayer, knowing that God knows who we are, knows each sorrow, each heartache, each weakness, and yet he loves us completely. In the temple, we approach Him who has the power to forgive. The temple *is* a house of forgiveness. In Solomon's ancient dedicatory prayer, he speaks movingly of this. Read it again in Chronicles and be inspired by it (2 Chronicles 6). This dedicatory prayer helps us understand that the temple is a place where we come to look inward and find our own shortcomings. We can rise above them and stand tall, and He will forgive our sins. Each time we go to the temple it can be a time of repentance, an opportunity to turn our lives around. Does this give us power? Yes. It gives me the power to leave yesterday behind, get up in the morning, and try again. To keep going forward. To know that I can be better. It has been said that through the ordinances of the temple we actually have our natures changed to become like God.

As we grow in spiritual power through temple participation, we will have more peace in our homes and love in our relationships.

President Hinckley has said: "Keep the temple as busy or busier than it has been. The Lord will bless you and you will be happier. I make a promise to you that every time you come to the temple you will be a better man or woman when you leave than you were when you came. That is a promise. I believe it with all my heart" ("President Hinckley Addresses 15,000 in Laie," *Church News*, 28 February 2000).

Keep thinking power. As you watch the downward spiral of our society as portrayed in the media, do you feel helpless? George Q. Cannon taught that the construction of temples "lessens the power of Satan on the earth and increases the power of God and Godliness, [and] moves the heavens in mighty power in our behalf" (*Gospel Truth*, ed. Jerreld L. Newquist [Salt Lake City: Deseret Book, 1987], 366).

That means that with every announcement of and dedication of a temple reported in the newspaper, we can know that we are making headway against the forces of evil.

———

See Virginia H. Pearce, "'I Will Manifest Myself to My People,'" Arise and Shine Forth (Salt Lake City: Deseret Book, 2001), 262.

A PROMISE

~~

Ezra Taft Benson

I would like to express the hope we all have for you, which is so real, that you will be exalted in the highest degree of glory in the celestial kingdom and that you will enter into the new and everlasting covenant of marriage.

Dear sisters, never lose sight of this sacred goal. Prayerfully prepare for it and live for it. Be married the Lord's way. Temple marriage is a gospel ordinance of exaltation. Our Father in Heaven wants each of his daughters to have this eternal blessing.

Therefore, don't trifle away your happiness by involvement with someone who cannot take you worthily to the temple. Make a decision now that this is the place where you will marry.

———

Ezra Taft Benson, who served as secretary of agriculture under U.S. president Dwight D. Eisenhower, was ordained an apostle in 1943 and sustained as president of the Church in 1985. He and his wife, Flora Amussen Benson, became the parents of six children. President Benson died in 1994 at the age of ninety-four.

To leave that decision until a romantic involvement develops is to take a risk the importance of which you cannot now fully calculate.

I also recognize that not all women in the Church will have an opportunity for marriage and motherhood in mortality. But if those of you in this situation are worthy and endure faithfully, you can be assured of all blessings from a kind and loving Heavenly Father—and I emphasize *all blessings*.

I assure you that if you have to wait even until the next life to be blessed with a choice companion, God will surely compensate you. Time is numbered only to man. God has your eternal perspective in mind.

All of the blessings of our Father in Heaven will be yours if you continue faithful, if you are true, and if you serve him and his children with all your heart, might, mind, and strength.

You are choice daughters of our Father in Heaven. You are jewels in his crown. Your virtue and purity make your price above rubies.

In the words of President David O. McKay, "A beautiful, modest, gracious woman is creation's masterpiece. When to these virtues a woman possesses as guiding stars in her life righteousness and godliness and an irresistible impulse and desire to make others happy, no one will question if she be classed among those who are truly great" (*Gospel Ideals* [Salt Lake City: The Improvement Era, 1953], 449).

———

See Ezra Taft Benson, "To the Single Adult Sisters of the Church," Ensign, November 1988, 96.

Six Lessons from the Temple

Carol B. Thomas

Why all this fuss about temples? Simply put, the purpose of temples "is to redeem all mankind who are obedient to the laws and commandments of God" (David B. Haight, "Personal Temple Worship," *Ensign*, May 1993, 23).

May I share a few things I have learned about temple worship.

Going to the temple often provides balance in our lives. After returning home, we have an increased sense of well-being; the influence of the Spirit can shield us from the frustrations of the world. Listen to this promise by President Gordon B. Hinckley: "If there were more temple work done in the Church, there would be less . . . selfishness, less . . . contention, less . . . demeaning [of] others. The whole Church would increasingly be lifted to greater heights of spirituality, love for one another, and obedience

---

Carol Burdett Thomas has served as a member of the general board of the Relief Society and as first counselor in the Young Women general presidency. She and her husband, D. Ray Thomas, are the parents of seven children.

to the commandments of God" (*Teachings of Gordon B. Hinckley* [Salt Lake City: Deseret Book, 1997], 622).

The spiritual atmosphere of the temple curbs our appetite for worldly things. When we attend frequently, we no longer have such a need to wear the latest fashion, and we are not so easily drawn to the entertainment of the world.

The temple is a place of revelation. Many years ago I was walking into the temple and in my mind I heard the words, *Learn public speaking.* I thought to myself, *When will I ever have need for public speaking?*

Over several months, I tried very inadequately to conjure up some enthusiasm to obey the prompting I had received. I even checked out a tape from the local library by a public speaker who admitted that his goal was to someday speak in the Mormon Tabernacle. I thought at the time, *I'll never be speaking in the Tabernacle!*

Elder John A. Widtsoe has said, "At the most unexpected moments, in or out of the temple will come to [us], as a revelation, the solution of the problems that vex [our lives]. . . . It is a place where revelations may be expected" ("Temple Worship," *Utah Genealogical and Historical Magazine,* April 1921, 63–64).

One of the biggest lessons I have learned is that Satan will try to keep us from going to the temple. Friends once shared with me that whenever they attend, they don't tell anybody they are going. They just jump into their cars and go, because if they don't, something is sure to happen to keep them away.

I remember reading of a warning given by the president of the Logan temple that Satan and his followers will "whisper in the ears of the people persuading them not to go to the Temple" ("Genealogical Department," *Church News,* 12 December 1936, 8). "Temple work brings so much resistance because it is the source of so much spiritual power to the Latter-day Saints" (Boyd K. Packer, "The Holy Temple," *Ensign,* February 1995, 36).

The Spirit of Elijah is brooding in the land. As we work with youth of the Church, we see they are being drawn to the temple.

In Nicaragua, a group of forty-nine young women and their leaders took two thousand names to the temple in Guatemala City. It took each girl a year to save enough money to go. These faithful young women rode a bus almost two days' journey through three countries to spend two or three days at the temple before returning home.

In another ward, young people have located the names of ten thousand ancestors as they have turned their hearts to their families. Where temples are available, we see youth doing baptisms for the dead, sometimes on an individual weekly basis.

In the temple, the Spirit of the Lord provides comfort and peace, especially during moments of despair. Not long ago, I met a thirty-five-year-old woman in the temple. As we visited, I asked if her husband was with her. With a look of tenderness in her eyes, she shared with me that he had died of a brain tumor three months before. The temple became her anchor: the Spirit found in the temple gave her comfort and peace, and perhaps her husband was there.

Spiritual strength and power come from temple worship. As servants of the living God, may we all press forward in this sacred temple work. And may we teach our children that as they spiritually prepare themselves for the temple, they may stand in the presence of the Lord.

———

See Carol B. Thomas, "Preparing Our Families for the Temple," Ensign, May 1999, 12.

THE GREATEST
BLESSINGS OF ETERNITY

J Ballard Washburn

President Howard W. Hunter said: "It is the deepest desire of
my heart to have every member of the Church *worthy* to enter the
temple" ("'Exceeding Great and Precious Promises,'" *Ensign*,
November 1994, 8; italics added).

The greatest blessings of eternity come to us through the
temple. God's greatest gift, eternal life, can only come to a man
and woman together. And every worthy person will someday have
this blessing. In marriage, a husband and wife enter into an order
of the priesthood called the new and everlasting covenant of marriage. This covenant includes a willingness to have children and
to teach them the gospel.

---

*J Ballard Washburn, a retired family doctor, has served as a member of the
Second Quorum of the Seventy and as president of the Arizona Phoenix
Mission. He and his wife, Barbara Harries Washburn, have served together
as president and matron of the Las Vegas Nevada Temple. They are the parents of ten children and many foster children.*

We go to the temple to make covenants, but we go home to keep the covenants that we have made. The home is the testing ground. The home is the place where we learn to be more Christlike. The home is the place where we learn to overcome selfishness and give ourselves in service to others.

I hope you will not think it simplistic to suggest that it is the "little things" like family prayer and family home evening that are important. Little things like a father helping his children say their nightly prayers and telling them a bedtime story instead of watching TV. Little things like making time in the family schedule for reading the scriptures. Little things like a husband being big enough to say, "Sweetheart, I'm sorry. I should not have said that. I'm going to do better." Or a mother saying to a child, "I'm sorry I became angry. Please forgive me." Yes, it is the little things that we do each day and each week that make the difference.

By keeping the temple covenants, all of God's children may be exalted. I say again that *we go to the temple to make the covenants, but we go home to keep those covenants.*

The story is told of Elder Boyd K. Packer: After traveling all over the world and seeing many exotic places, he was asked that if he could go anywhere in the world he wanted, where would he go. He replied, "I would go home." I feel the same way. If I were asked that same question, I would say, "I would go home and sit in a big rocking chair and take a couple of grandbabies in my arms and hope that a little of the heavenly dust they still have on them would rub off on me." I'm grateful for homes where we can go to learn how to love, how to share, how to be Christlike.

I am grateful for temples where we can go to be sealed together as families for eternity. I am grateful for temples, where we can go to pray and to worship, where we can call down the blessings of heaven upon our families. I am grateful for temples where we can go as families to strengthen the eternal bonds that will make us forever families, where we can go to do the great redemptive work for our forefathers who cannot do it for themselves, even as Jesus did for us what we cannot do for ourselves. I am grateful that God in his eternal wisdom has made these blessings available to all his children. Some, however, have to wait until the hereafter to enjoy these blessings. But all who live worthily will have every blessing. I testify that Jesus loved to go to the temple. Part of becoming more Christlike is to learn to love to go to the temple.

————

See J Ballard Washburn, "The Temple Is a Family Affair," Ensign, May 1995, 11.

A Place of Holiness

Elaine L. Jack

President Gordon B. Hinckley's tremendous temple-building effort has reminded us of the solemn responsibility to serve in the temple. He said, "In the house of the Lord there is tranquillity. Those who serve here know that they are dealing with matters of eternity. All are dressed in white. Speech is subdued. Thoughts are elevated.

"This is a sanctuary of service. Most of the work done in this sacred house is performed vicariously in behalf of those who have passed beyond the veil of death. I know of no other work to compare with it. It more nearly approaches the vicarious sacrifice of the Son of God in behalf of all mankind than any other work of which I am aware. Thanks is not expected from those who in the

Elaine L. Jack has served as general president of the Relief Society and as matron of the Cardston Alberta Temple. A native of Canada, she attended the University of Utah as an English major. She and her husband, Joseph E. Jack, are the parents of four sons.

world beyond become the beneficiaries of this consecrated service. It is a service of the living in behalf of the dead. It is a service which is of the very essence of selflessness" (*Teachings of Gordon B. Hinckley* [Salt Lake City: Deseret Book, 1997], 635).

Our hearts must be pure, for temple work speaks to the heart. We must prepare to attend the temple; we must honor our covenants; we must live worthy to receive his holy blessings. When we bring hearts that are pure, we are able to feel the power of the Lord's way of learning. Learn of him. Ponder over the experience. Do we rush home from the temple, falling back into the world and its patterns, or do we ponder our experience that we may understand? In 3 Nephi, the resurrected Lord instructs the people who have been with him, "Go ye unto your homes, and ponder upon the things which I have said, and ask of the Father, in my name, that ye may understand, and prepare your minds for the morrow, and I come unto you again" (3 Nephi 17:3). That is wise counsel for us as we return to our homes, having been instructed by the Lord in the temple—for he has told us, "by mine own voice or by the voice of my servants, it is the same" (D&C 1:38). May we pray to better grasp the covenants we have made; may we gain a greater understanding of the work we have done; may we sustain the spirit of tranquillity so abundant in the temple.

In the Doctrine and Covenants, the Lord explains that in the temple we are "endowed with power from on high" (D&C 38:32). The Lord then reveals, "I have a great work laid up in store" (v. 33). That endowment of power allows us to use our talents, gifts, and personal abilities with greater influence and increased intelligence to further the kingdom of God. This I know—we mature spiritually in the temple. I had the great privilege of participating in the rededication of the Cardston Temple in 1991. I will always remember the sacredness of that occasion. At the rededication, President Howard W. Hunter, then president of the Quorum of the Twelve Apostles, spoke directly of the power of the temple to change people's lives: "The temple is the place where one takes his bearing on the universe" ("Temples like 'No Other Places in World,'" *Church News,* 29 June 1991,10). Said Elder Boyd K. Packer, "May we find our way home through the rest of our lives to that home where there will be no parting" ("Temples," *Church News,* 29 June 1991,10).

The Lord says, "Therefore are they before the throne of God, and serve him day and night in his temple: and he that sitteth on the throne shall dwell among them" (Revelation 7:15). The Lord is aware of temple service. In Revelation is found clear assurance: "I know thy works, and charity, and service, and faith, and thy patience, and thy works; and the last to be more than the first"

(Revelation 2:19). To me, this means that when we do our work with charity and faith and patience, the Lord will magnify it.

We have as our purpose to come unto Christ. We come unto Christ in the temple. His spirit is there. The temple ceremony confirms the importance of each individual as a child of God, of the eternity of the marriage relationship, and of going on to greater glory. It brings comfort and a surety of a better life. I am profoundly moved at the conclusion of each session when I am reminded of the ultimate blessings promised by the Savior. Each is a blessing I fervently seek. Each is a blessing I receive in no other place. The temple is where the Lord brings the greatest measure of peace and hope and understanding and joy.

I love the temple, and I love the Lord, whose work this is.

See Elaine L. Jack, "It Is Thy House, a Place of Holiness," address delivered at Women's Conference, Brigham Young University, Provo, Utah, May 2001.

OUR ONLY CHANCE

Sheri Dew

"In the gift of his Son hath God prepared a more excellent way" (Ether 12:11). The Savior isn't our last chance; He is our only chance. Our only chance to overcome self-doubt and catch a vision of who we may become. Our only chance to repent and have our sins washed clean. Our only chance to purify our hearts, subdue our weaknesses, and avoid the adversary. Our only chance to obtain redemption and exaltation. Our only chance to find peace and happiness in this life and eternal life in the world to come.

The Lord knows the way because He *is* the way and is our only chance for successfully negotiating mortality. His atonement makes available all of the power, peace, light, and strength that we need to deal with life's challenges—those ranging from our own

---

Sheri Dew has served as second counselor in the Relief Society general presidency. A graduate of Brigham Young University in history and a best-selling author, she serves as president of Deseret Book Company.

mistakes and sins to trials over which we have no control but for which we still feel pain.

The Lord has promised to heal our broken hearts and "to set at liberty them that are bruised" (Luke 4:18); to give power to the faint, to heal the wounded soul, and to turn our weakness into strength (Isaiah 40:29; Jacob 2:8; Ether 12:27); to take upon Him our pains and sicknesses, to blot out our transgressions if we repent, and loose the bands of death (Alma 7:11–13). He promised that if we will build our lives upon His rock, the devil will have no power over us (Helaman 5:12). And He has vowed that He will never leave us or forsake us (Hebrews 13:5). There is simply no mortal equivalent. Not in terms of commitment, power, or love. He is our only chance.

Our responsibility is to learn to draw upon the power of the Atonement. Otherwise we walk through mortality relying solely on our own strength. And to do that is to invite the frustration of failure and to refuse the most resplendent gift in time or eternity. "For what doth it profit a man if a gift is bestowed . . . and he receive not the gift?" (D&C 88:33). The Lord is our advocate, and He "knoweth the weakness of man and how to succor them who are tempted" (D&C 62:1). In other words, He knows how to succor *all* of us. But *we* activate the power of the Atonement in our lives. We do this by first believing in Him, by repenting, by obeying His commandments, by partaking of sacred ordinances and keeping covenants, and by seeking after Him in fasting and prayer, in the scriptures, and in the temple.

Is it possible to be happy when life is hard? To feel peace amid uncertainty and hope in the midst of cynicism? Is it possible to change, to shake off old habits and become new again? Is it possible to live with integrity and purity in a world that no longer values the virtues that distinguish the followers of Christ?

Yes. The answer is yes because of Jesus Christ, whose atonement ensures that we need not bear the burdens of mortality alone. There is nothing this confused world needs more, nothing that inspires a greater sense of well-being, nothing that has greater power to strengthen families than the gospel of Jesus Christ. President Howard W. Hunter said, "Whatever Jesus lays his hands upon lives. If Jesus lays his hands upon a marriage, it lives. If he is allowed to lay his hands on the family, it lives" (Conference Report, October 1979, 93). The Savior will do for *each* of us what He has promised to do—*if* we will have faith in Him and receive His gift.

Through the years I, like you, have experienced pressures and disappointments that would have crushed me had I not been able to draw upon a source of wisdom and strength far greater than my own. He has never forgotten or forsaken me, and I have come to know for myself that Jesus *is* the Christ and that this is His Church. With Ammon I say, "[For] who can glory too much in the Lord? Yea, who can say too much of his great power, and of his mercy . . . ? Behold, . . . I cannot say the smallest part which I feel" (Alma 26:16). I testify that in this, the twilight of the dispensation of the fulness of times, when Lucifer is working overtime to jeopardize our journey home and to separate us from the Savior's atoning power, the only answer for *any* of us is Jesus Christ.

May we recommit to seek after this Jesus, of whom the prophets have testified. May we yoke ourselves to Him, draw liberally upon the matchless power of His atonement, and rise up as sons and daughters of God and shake off the world. To "those who will have him to be their God" (1 Nephi 17:40), the Lord has extended a magnificent promise: "I will go before your face. I will be on your right hand and on your left, and my Spirit shall be in your hearts, and mine angels round about you, to bear you up" (D&C 84:88). Jesus Christ is our only chance. He will show us the way because He *is* the way.

See Sheri Dew, "Our Only Chance," Ensign, *May 1999, 66.*

THE JOURNEY HAS A JOYFUL END

Stephen D. Nadauld

It should be an easy matter to place our trust in someone who is omnipotent and omniscient. But we are reluctant, and we struggle. We struggle because of our pride. We struggle because of our imperfections.

There is no more eloquent statement of that struggle and resulting trust than that expressed by Nephi in 2 Nephi 4. He begins by describing feelings that we have all had:

"Notwithstanding the great goodness of the Lord, in showing me his great and marvelous works, my heart exclaimeth: O wretched man that I am! Yea, my heart sorroweth because of my flesh; my soul grieveth because of mine iniquities. . . . And when

Stephen D. Nadauld, a professor at the Marriott School of Management at Brigham Young University, has served as a member of the Second Quorum of the Seventy. He and his wife, Margaret D. Nadauld, who has served as Young Women general president, are the parents of seven children.

I desire to rejoice, my heart groaneth because of my sins" (2 Nephi 4:17–19).

Then he exclaims, "Nevertheless, I know in whom I have trusted. My God hath been my support; he hath led me . . . ; and he hath preserved me. . . . He hath filled me with his love. . . . He hath confounded mine enemies. . . . He hath heard my cry . . . ; he hath given me knowledge by visions" (2 Nephi 4:20–23).

In other words, Nephi is rehearsing the evidence of things both seen and unseen. And so he observes: "Awake, my soul! . . . Rejoice, O my heart. . . . Do not anger again. . . . Do not slacken my strength. . . . Rejoice, O my heart, and cry unto the Lord, and say: O Lord, I will praise thee forever; yea, my soul will rejoice in thee, my God, and the rock of my salvation." Then we read this phrase of beautiful visual imagery: "O Lord, wilt thou encircle me around in the robe of thy righteousness!" Nephi finishes with these final thoughts: "O Lord, I have trusted in thee, and I will trust in thee forever. I will not put my trust in the arm of flesh. . . . Yea, I know that God will give liberally to him that asketh. Yea, my God will give me, if I ask not amiss; therefore I will lift up my voice unto thee; yea, I will cry unto thee, my God, the rock of my righteousness. Behold, my voice shall forever ascend up unto thee, my rock and mine everlasting God. Amen" (2 Nephi 4:28–30, 33–35).

What an inspiring expression of trust in the Lord. Nephi rehearses his experience with the Lord and reaffirms his trust. We would do well to ponder at length this extraordinary passage. I call to your attention one particular phrase. Nephi says, "I will not put my trust in the arm of flesh" (2 Nephi 4:34).

How we wish we could see into the future to know the outcome of every troublesome decision and to arrive at the destination without having to make the journey. Many of you pay your tithing, read the scriptures, keep yourselves morally clean, and pray with real intent. And yet you may experience periods of disappointment and heartache as you face the challenges of life. This is normal; your faith is not misplaced. Remember the words of the hymn, "Be still, my soul: Thy best, thy heav'nly Friend / Through thorny ways leads to a joyful end" (*Hymns* [Salt Lake City: The Church of Jesus Christ of Latter-day Saints, 1985], no. 124).

The journey does have a joyful end. That is the message of the plan of redemption. Christ said, "Be of good cheer; I have overcome the world" (John 16:33). Faith in the plan of redemption and its outcomes leads to keeping the commandments. Faith and trust provide the foundation for a happy and productive life. You will be grateful for a full reservoir of faith and trust to see you through life's experiences.

So put away your fears, put away your anxieties, put away your sins and your pettiness. Believe in God's plan; trust in him. Put not your trust in the arm of flesh, lean not on your own understanding, but be believing, desiring that the Lord will encircle you about in the robe of his righteousness. Study to increase your faith, study the Atonement, study the Resurrection, study the plan of redemption, and study the relationship among faith and trust and humility.

With faith and trust firmly in place, a wonderful thing can happen. You can set aside your self-absorption, quiet your anxieties and fears, and fill your souls with love. The Savior's message is clear: understanding the doctrine should lead to practical application. Practice serving, practice lifting and building, strengthen others, provide assurances, and rehearse the evidence.

What a remarkable transformation takes place when we allow our faith to lead to trust. The most amazing thing will happen. Our faith, combined with trust, kindles *love*. Love of the Savior, love of our fellowman, love for those near and dear to us. Love that provides sweetness, true joy, the giving of oneself for others.

I witness to you that God's plan of redemption is a true plan of happiness. I add my assurance that Jesus Christ is our Savior. He is our Redeemer. He fulfilled his role as the Messiah, the Anointed One, who atoned for our sins. The Resurrection is a reality. We can live eternally with a loving Heavenly Father. May we increase our faith, reaffirm our trust, and rekindle our love.

———

See Stephen D. Nadauld, "Learning to Be Like the Lord," Ensign, December 1995, 7.

ETERNAL PROGRESSION

~

Elaine L. Jack

Before we came to this earth, we shouted for joy at the opportunity to take this leap of faith in our eternal progression. This is a journey made up of many steps. Our progress on this journey is determined by recognizing the straight and narrow path, having an eternal perspective, and acting accordingly.

Remember, our eternal progression is the very essence of our earthly existence. It is the Lord's plan to get us all the way home to our Father in Heaven. This I know: Each of us can get there from here.

President Spencer W. Kimball promised, "It may seem a little difficult at first, but when a person begins to catch a vision of the true work, when he begins to see something of eternity in its true

---

Elaine L. Jack has served as general president of the Relief Society and as matron of the Cardston Alberta Temple. A native of Canada, she attended the University of Utah as an English major. She and her husband, Joseph E. Jack, are the parents of four sons.

perspective, the blessings begin to far outweigh the cost of leaving 'the world' behind" ("The False Gods We Worship," *Ensign*, June 1976, 6).

Some of our steps come in learning that the path is indeed straight and narrow. The concept of a straight path intrigues me. So often we go around in a circle, spinning our spiritual wheels while only our temporal treads hit the road. That seems out of step and out of balance with the way the Lord intended. We have knowledge and spiritual power; such momentum far exceeds anything the world has to offer. Putting off till tomorrow is to fall behind, step backward, and open the door to the subtle influences of Satan. "There is no such thing as standing still in the eternal work of our God" (George Q. Cannon, *Millennial Star*, 23 February 1899, 117).

Elder Neal A. Maxwell has said, "There are no separate paths back to that heavenly home. Just one straight and narrow way, at the end of which, though we arrive trailing tears, we shall at once be 'drenched in joy'" ("The Women of God," *Ensign*, May 1978, 11).

Indeed, the path is not soft, green grass; it is not without hardship and heartache. It is often an uphill climb strewn with rocks, many of them in the shape of mighty boulders. We can't predict what our challenges will be because our lives are all different. Though the path is narrow, our moves are not scripted. There are diversions which attempt to lure us from the straight and narrow. It is our covenants that are the road signs to eternal life. Just as it is more difficult to read the signs on the main road from a side street, so too it is more difficult to hear the still, small voice of warning when we have distanced ourselves from our covenants.

When the Lord says "walk with me" (Moses 6:34), he is asking us to become more spiritual by being obedient to his word. Developing spirituality is critical to our eternal progress.

Our prophet has spoken for the Lord in our day, and his messages have been explicit: rid your heart of pride; read the Book of Mormon every day. We are told to attend Church meetings, work hard in callings, go to the temple, be generous in offerings to the Lord, hold family home evening, and visit one another. But simply being there does not sanctify us; statistics do not drive eternal progression. Still, we cannot ignore that being in the right place at the right time will put us in a frame of mind to learn, in an environment where the Lord's influence is invited and strong.

We know why we are here. When we are on the path, we can feel it. The fruits of eternal progress are manifest in joy, peace, love, hope, increased confidence in the Lord. Though the path is narrow, it is sure. It is on this path that we testify daily of our love for the Lord, his children, his church, his counsel, and the richness of his blessings. By our good works we magnify what is mighty in us all, one step at a time, one day at a time, all the time.

We know the path; in fact, we know it well. The prophet Nephi promised, "If ye shall press forward, feasting upon the word of Christ, and endure to the end, behold, thus saith the Father: Ye shall have eternal life" (2 Nephi 31:20). May it be so.

———

See Elaine L. Jack, "Walk with Me," Ensign, May 1994, 15.

THE QUALITY OF ETERNAL LIFE

~~

Wm. Grant Bangerter

Is there a purpose in such a temporary existence? Some say there is not. The great question of Job haunts us all: "If a man die, shall he live again?" (Job 14:14). Of course he will! The answer is found in the doctrine of eternal life. It is the gospel of Jesus Christ, the good news, the glad tidings.

Joseph Smith tells us that "happiness is the object and design of our existence; and will be the end thereof, if we pursue the path which leads to it" (*Teachings of the Prophet Joseph Smith*, sel. Joseph Fielding Smith [Salt Lake City: Deseret Book, 1938], 255).

Wm. Grant Bangerter has served as a member of the First Quorum of the Seventy and as a member of the presidency of the Seventy. He also served for ten years as executive director of the Temple Department of the Church. He and his wife, Geraldine Hamblin Bangerter, served together as president and matron of the Jordan River Utah Temple. They are the parents of ten children.

There are several fundamentals which those who seek to enjoy quality in their eternal existence would want to consider.

We begin by knowing of Jesus Christ and determining to follow him. Peter said: "Repent, and be baptized every one of you in the name of Jesus Christ for the remission of sins, and ye shall receive the gift of the Holy Ghost" (Acts 2:38).

Then, we "press forward with a steadfastness in Christ . . . and endure to the end, [and] thus saith the Father: Ye shall have eternal life" (2 Nephi 31:20). We are to take upon us his name and always remember him and keep his commandments (Moroni 4–5; D&C 20:77–79). That seems to be keeping our repentance up to date.

Now comes the call to serve. We serve God and our fellowmen. The parable of the Good Samaritan came in answer to the lawyer's question: "What shall I do to obtain eternal life? . . . Thou shalt love the Lord thy God . . . and thy neighbour as thyself" (Luke 10:25–27).

To receive the blessings that accompany this service we are given the priesthood and its power. It has been called "the Holy Priesthood, after the Order of the Son of God" (D&C 107:3). "And without the ordinances thereof, and the authority of the priesthood, . . . no man can see the face of God, even the Father, and live" (D&C 84:21–22). Now, the way of God leads us to the temple. These sacred edifices fulfill an eternal purpose.

Just as the ancient Israelites looked to the temple for their salvation, even so will those who are in earnest find in the temple the pathway to the presence of the Father and the Son. There they receive holy ordinances as they covenant to keep the commandments.

Immortality, or the resurrection, will happen to us all. It is an unearned benefit made possible through the grace, or free gift, of Christ. Eternal life in happiness and glory in association with those we love will be the reward only of those who exercise faith in Jesus Christ through obedience to his commandments.

———

See Wm. Grant Bangerter, "The Quality of Eternal Life," Ensign, *November 1988, 80.*

We Make the Choice

~~

Bruce R. McConkie

Death can be comforting and sweet and precious, or it can thrust upon us all the agonies and sulphurous burnings of an endless hell. And we—each of us individually—make the choice as to which it shall be.

If we are to place death in its proper perspective in the eternal scheme of things, we must first learn the purposes of life. We must know whence we came, Whose we are, and why He placed us here. Only then can we envision whither we shall yet go in the providences of Him who made us.

We know, because the Lord has revealed it in this our day, that we are the spirit children of an exalted, glorified Being, a Holy Man who has a body of flesh and bones and who is our Father in heaven.

―――――

Bruce R. McConkie served as a member of the Quorum of the Twelve Apostles from 1972 until his death in 1985 at the age of sixty-nine. A prolific and inspiring writer, he and his wife, Amelia Smith McConkie, became the parents of nine children.

We know that the name of the kind of life he lives is *eternal life* and that it consists of living in the family unit and of possessing all power, all might, and all dominion.

We know that he ordained and established the plan of salvation to enable us to advance and progress from our spirit state, to the same state of glory, honor, and exaltation which he himself possesses.

We know that the Father's plan called for the creation of this earth, where we could dwell as mortals, receive bodies made of the dust of the earth, and undergo the tests and trials which now face us.

We know that this plan of salvation included provisions for the fall of man, with its consequent temporal and spiritual death, for a redemption from death through the atoning sacrifice of the Son of God, and for an inheritance of eternal life for all the obedient.

We know that this great plan of progression called for a *birth* which would provide a mortal tabernacle for our eternal spirits, and for a *death* which would free those spirits from the frailties, diseases, and weaknesses of mortality.

And may I say that this life never was intended to be easy. It is a probationary estate in which we are tested physically, mentally, morally, and spiritually. We are subject to disease and decay. We are attacked by cancer, leprosy, and contagious diseases.

We suffer pain and sorrow and afflictions. Disasters strike; floods sweep away our homes; famines destroy our food; plagues and wars fill our graves with dead bodies and our broken homes with sorrow.

We are called upon to choose between the revealed word of God and the soul-destroying postulates of the theoretical sciences. Temptations, the lusts of the flesh, evils of every sort—all these are part of the plan—and must be faced by every person privileged to undergo the experiences of mortality.

The testing processes of mortality are for all men, saints and sinners alike. Sometimes the tests and trials of those who have received the gospel far exceed any imposed upon worldly people. Abraham was called upon to sacrifice his only son. Lehi and his family left their lands and wealth to live in a wilderness. Saints in all ages have been commanded to lay all that they have upon the altar, sometimes even their very lives.

As to the individual trials and problems that befall any of us, all we need say is that in the wisdom of him who knows all things, and who does all the things well, all of us are given the particular and specific tests that we need in our personal situations. It is to us, his Saints, that the Lord speaks when he says: "I will prove you in all things, whether you will abide in my covenant, even unto death, that you may be found worthy. For if ye will not abide in my covenant ye are not worthy of me" (D&C 98:14–15).

We shouted for joy at the privilege of becoming mortal because without the tests of mortality there could be no eternal life. We now sing praises to the great Redeemer for the privilege of passing from this life because without death and the resurrection we could not be raised in immortal glory and gain eternal life.

When the faithful Saints depart from this life, they "are received into a state of happiness, which is called paradise, a state of rest, a state of peace, where they shall rest from all their troubles and from all care, and sorrow" (Alma 40:12), and they remain in this state until the day of their resurrection.

When the wicked and ungodly depart from this life, they continue in their wickedness and rebellion. "That same spirit which doth possess your bodies at the time ye go out of this life," the scripture says, "that same spirit will have power to possess your body in that eternal world" (Alma 34:34).

"Ye must press forward with a steadfastness in Christ," Nephi said to members of the Church, "having a perfect brightness of hope, and a love of God and of all men. Wherefore, if ye shall press forward, feasting upon the word of Christ, and endure to the end, behold, thus saith the Father: Ye shall have eternal life" (2 Nephi 31:20). That is to say—all the faithful Saints, all of those who have endured to the end, depart this life with the absolute guarantee of eternal life.

There is no equivocation, no doubt, no uncertainty in our minds. Those who have been true and faithful in this life will not fall by the wayside in the life to come. If they keep their covenants here and now and depart this life firm and true in the testimony of our blessed Lord, they shall come forth with an inheritance of eternal life.

We do not mean to say that those who die in the Lord, and who are true and faithful in this life, must be perfect in all things when they go into the next sphere of existence. There was only one perfect man—the Lord Jesus whose Father was God.

There have been many righteous souls who have attained relative degrees of perfection, and there have been great hosts of faithful people who have kept the faith, and lived the law, and departed this life with the full assurance of an eventual inheritance of eternal life.

There are many things they will do and must do, even beyond the grave, to merit the fulness of the Father's kingdom in that final glorious day when the great King shall say unto them, "Come, ye blessed of my Father, inherit the kingdom prepared for you from the foundation of the world" (Matthew 25:34).

But what we are saying is that when the Saints of God chart a course of righteousness, when they gain sure testimonies of the truth and divinity of the Lord's work, when they keep the commandments, when they overcome the world, when they put first in their lives the things of God's kingdom, when they do all these things, and then depart this life—though they have not yet become perfect—they shall nonetheless gain eternal life in our Father's kingdom; and eventually they shall be perfect as God their Father and Christ his Son are perfect.

Is it any wonder that the scriptures say: "Precious in the sight of the Lord is the death of his saints"? (Psalm 116:15). Truly, such is precious, wondrous, and glorious, for when the Saints die, added souls have assured themselves of exaltation with Him who provided the way for them to advance and progress and become like Him.

———

See Bruce R. McConkie, "The Dead Who Die in the Lord," Ensign, November 1976, 106.

INDEX

～ F ～

Faith: finding peace through, 10, 174; as source of strength, 31; as necessary for making choices, 189; in plan of happiness, 248

Family: disintegration of, 97; importance of, 98–99; helping members of, 105; making time for, 108, 236; loving nature of children in, 111–12; Proclamation on the, 121, 217–18; joy in, 126–27, 133; leading, with love, 131–33; parenting in, 134–37; difficulties with, 193; roles of men and women in, 196–98. *See also* Home, Marriage, Mother

Father in Heaven. *See* God

Faust, James E., on womanhood, 122

Fear, 25

Frankl, Victor, on agency, 189

Franklin, Benjamin, on time, 169

Friendship, in marriage, 102–4

～ G ～

Gender: as eternal identity, 121; roles of men and women, 196–98

General conference, 78

God: love of, 10, 45, 195; as our Father, 18–19, 134–35, 258; dedicating our lives to, 20–22; turning to, in times of trial, 26, 73–76, 174; shares our burdens, 32; returning home to, 63; is aware of us, 161–62, 171–72, 226; trusting in, 174, 184–86, 246–50; grants us strength to bear

adversity, 190; prophet the mouthpiece of, 217; inviting influence of, 253; wisdom of, 260

Grant, Heber J., on motherhood, 106–7

～ H ～

Haight, David B.: on sustaining the prophet, 211; on purpose of temples, 231

Hearts: desires of, 20–22, 109, 122; change of, 67–68; purity of, 224

Hinckley, Gordon B.: on reaching potential, 12; on finding fulfillment in family, 15; on service, 41, 147; on prayer, 54; as God's mouthpiece, 78–79; on Holy Ghost, 90; on parenting, 136; gives guidance to women, 145; on doing good, 156; on calling of women, 202; on sustaining leaders, 212; on Church membership in our day, 219; on temples, 224, 227, 231–32, 238

Holland, Jeffrey R., on home, 15

Holy Ghost: comforts in times of fear, 26; guidance of, 40; communications of, 84; description of, 90–93

Home: building the ideal, 113–14; happiness in, 115; blessing of, 236–37

Hunger, 150–51

Hunter, Howard W.: on temples, 240; on saving power of Christ, 244

Hymns, 86

～ I ～

In His Steps, 149–50

Sheldon, Charles, 149–50

Smith, Emma, 146

Smith, Joseph: on charity, 38; on gaining a testimony of the scriptures, 60–61; on Relief Society, 146; on priesthood, 218–19; on purpose of life, 255

Smith, Joseph F., on success, 105

Smith, Lucy Mack: on service, 42; on her search for religion, 192

Smith, Mary Fielding, 29–31

Smoot, Mary Ellen: on mission as daughters of Zion, 1; on purpose of Relief Society Declaration, 2

Snow, Eliza R.: on protection of Holy Ghost, 89; on covenants, 258

Snow, Lorenzo, on privilege of Holy Ghost, 89

~ T ~

Talmage, James E., on prayer, 81

Temple: man as, 68, 122–23; marriage in, 100; obtain recommend for, 135–36; and fulness of the gospel, 223; blessing of, worship, 224, 241; purpose of, 231–34; ponder experiences in, 239

Ten virgins, 151

Testimony: necessary to teach our children, 106; as a strength, 191; of prophet, 211

Time: using, well, 169; for family, 188; for temple worship, 226–27. *See also* Priorities, Procrastination

Tree of life, 181

Trials: turning to God in, 26, 73; faith in, 31; finding joy amidst, 127–29; necessity of, 183–84; experienced by all, 260

~ V ~

Van Gogh, Vincent, 26–27

~ W ~

Widtsoe, John A.: on equality of men and women, 195–96, 259; on revelation through temple worship, 232

Woodruff, Wilford, on need for living prophet, 215

Womanhood: qualities of, 122; celebration of, 129

Women: need of, to please others, 26–27; as daughters of God, 68–69; worth of, 141; various roles of, 192; calling of, 201; influence of, 203; blessing promised to unmarried, 229

Women of God: characteristics of, 121–25; need for, 138–41; different from women of world, 198

~ Y ~

Young, Brigham: on putting God first, 21; on becoming perfect, 28; on Holy Ghost, 90